A Summer of Psalms

by Karyn Henley

Child Sensitive Communication, LLC
Nashville, TN

Day By Day Devotions: A Summer of Psalms by Karyn Henley

Copyright © 2010 Karyn Henley. All rights reserved.

Exclusively administered by Child Sensitive Communication, LLC.

> Child Sensitive Communication, LLC
> PO Box 150806
> Nashville, TN 37215-0806
> www.KarynHenley.com

No part of this publication may be reproduced, stored in a retrieval system, or transmitted in any form or by any means (electronic, mechanical, photocopying, recording, or otherwise) without prior written permission.

Cover photo © Jupiter.com. All rights reserved. Used by permission.

Interior illustrations by Marlene Ekman. Interior illustrations © 1998 Karyn Henley. All rights reserved. Exclusively administered by Child Sensitive Communication, LLC.

Bible story excerpts are taken from the *Day By Day Kid's Bible*, © 1998 Karyn Henley. All rights reserved. Exclusively administered by Child Sensitive Communication, LLC.

ISBN 978-1-933803-39-5

Contents

A Letter to Readers	7
1. Giants *Psalm 56:1-4, 13*	8
2. Like an Olive Tree *Psalm 52*	10
3. Caves *Psalm 142*	12
4. Taking Grain from Barns *Psalm 63*	14
5. Oasis *Psalm 57*	16
6. City Walls *Psalm 51*	18
7. Becoming a King *Psalm 3*	20
8. The Ark *Psalm 105:1-3; 96:1-8*	22
9. Tents *Psalm 18*	24
10. God's Angel *Psalm 34:1-10*	26
11. School *Psalm 34:11-22*	28
12. Shepherds *Psalm 23*	30
13. Who Was Korah? *Psalm 46*	32
14. Rocky Places *Psalm 61*	34
15. Forts *Psalm 62*	36
16. Hair *Psalm 71*	38
17. Who is Asaph? *Psalm 77, by Asaph*	40
18. Sickness *Psalm 91*	42
19. Afraid of the Sea *Psalm 95:1-7*	44
20. Alarm Clocks *Psalm 108, by David*	46
21. Hills and High Places *Psalm 121*	48
22. Roads and Highways *Psalm 143*	50
23. Healthy Plants and Strong Pillars *Psalm 144*	52

Table of Contents

24. Rivers — 54
    Psalm 1

25. Common Animals — 56
    Psalm 36

26. Common Plants — 58
    Psalm 37:1-11

27. Pits and Marshes — 60
    Psalm 40:1-10

28. Riddles — 62
    Psalm 49

29. Promises and Vows — 64
    Psalm 50

30. Shoes — 66
    Psalm 73

31. Shields — 68
    Psalm 84, by Korah's Family

32. A Very Old Song — 70
    Psalm 90

33. Music — 72
    Psalm 92

34. Trading, Buying, and Selling — 74
    Psalm 112

35. Nations and Their "Gods" — 76
    Psalm 115

36. Wild Animals — 78
    Psalm 8

37. Ships — 80
    Psalm 107:1-31

38. Up in the Sky — 82
    Psalm 19

39. Doorkeepers — 84
    Psalm 24

40. Deserts — 86
    Psalm 29

41. Storehouses — 88
    Psalm 33:1-11

42. Armies — 90
    Psalm 33:12-22

43. Harvest — 92
    Psalm 65

44. Prayer — 94
    Psalm 66:16-20

45. Clothes — 96
    Psalm 93

46. Judges — 98
    Psalm 94:1-15

47. The Poor — 100
    Psalm 86

48. Horns — 102
    Psalm 98

49. Zion — 104
    Psalm 99:1-5

50. Palaces *Psalm 100*	106	62. Towers *Psalm 122*	130
51. Clans *Psalm 103*	108	63. Snares and Traps *Psalm 124*	132
52. Winds *Psalm 104:1-16*	110	64. The Worship House *Psalm 138*	134
53. A Moon Calendar *Psalm 104:17-35*	112	65. Books *Psalm 139*	136
54. Servants and Slaves *Psalm 113*	114	66. Praise *Psalm 145*	138
55. The Law *Psalm 119:1-16*	116	67. Weather *Psalm 148*	140
56. Money *Psalm 119:65-72*	118	68. Dancing *Psalm 150*	142
57. Eyes *Psalm 119:81-96*	120	69. Chariots *Psalm 20*	144
58. Lamps *Psalm 119:97-112*	122	70. Coming Back Home *Psalm 126*	146
59. Guards *Psalm 119:113-128*	124	71. Horses and Mules *Psalm 32*	148
60. Beds and Blankets *Psalm 149:1-5, 9*	126	72. Carrying Water *Psalm 42*	150
61. Rocks and Stones *Psalm 118:1, 5-6, 8-16, 19-24, 28-29*	128	73. Neighbors *Psalm 101*	152

74. Eating *Psalm 111*	154
75. Guards in the Night *Psalm 130*	156
76. Babies *Psalm 131*	158
77. Blind and Needy *Psalm 146*	160
78. Perfume *Psalm 45*	162
79. Joy Songs *Psalm 47*	164
80. Sharing Stories *Psalm 44:1-8*	166

A Letter to Readers

Dear reader,

Have you ever wondered what it might have been like to live in Bible times? The readings in this book will give you some idea of what life was like in the time of David, the shepherd boy who became king. That was long before Jesus' time. So if you have read *Day by Day Devotions with Jesus in Ancient Palestine*, you may notice that some things changed between the time of David and the time of Jesus. One thing that changed was the name of the country. In Jesus' time, it was called Palestine. In David's time, it was the land of Canaan. Not long after David, the land was ruled by two kings, with one part called Israel and the other part called Judah. But in this book, I call the country its old name: Canaan.

Something else changed between the time of David and the time of Jesus. Before David's time, the people who followed God were called Israelites and then Hebrews. By Jesus' time, they were called the Jews or the Jewish people. In this book, I call them Hebrews.

All the Bible readings in this book are from the Psalms as they are told in the *Day by Day Kids' Bible*. A psalm is a song. Many of these songs were written by David. In the Bible, some of the songs tell us when they were written, so I have put them first along with the stories that go with them. Not all songs have stories. But they all talk about something interesting.

So imagine that you lived at David's time.
And enjoy!

May God bless you!

Karyn Henley

WEEK 1

 Monday

Giants

Writings from long ago in Egypt say that giants lived in the land of Canaan, the land God promised to give to the Hebrews. So if you lived with the Hebrews in Egypt or traveled with them to Canaan, the Promised Land, you would hear about giants. Giants were extra tall, extra strong people. There were whole families of giants. Some of them were still around in David's time.

The giant we know by name was Goliath, who was nine feet tall. His spear was huge and heavy. Just the iron tip weighed 15 pounds. Goliath's sword was probably large too, but it was not too big for David to handle, as this story shows:

King Saul was chasing David. David ran to a priest in the town of Nob. "Do you have a spear or sword here?" asked David. "I was in a hurry. So I didn't bring mine."

"Goliath's sword is the only one I have," said the priest. "Take it if you want it."

"There is no other sword like it," said David. "I'll take it." He knew he had to get away from Saul. So he took the sword and ran to the town of Gath.

The king of Gath had servants. They said, "Isn't this David? He is the one the song is about. The song says Saul killed a few thousand. But David killed tens of thousands."

David heard what they said. He was afraid the king of Gath would be angry at him. So David wrote this song there:

(1 Samuel 21:1-12)

Psalm 56:1-4, 13

Be kind to me, God.
Men are chasing me.
All day these proud men fight.
I will trust in you when I am afraid.
I praise your word.
I trust in God.
I will not be afraid.
What can people do to me?
I can walk with you, God.
You give light to my life.

To read about giants in the Bible, try Genesis 6:4; Numbers 13:30-33; Deut. 2:10; 9:1-3; and 2 Samuel 21:16-22.

Tuesday

Like an Olive Tree

King Saul sent for the priest of Nob. He came and brought all the priests of Nob with him.

"Why did you turn against me?" Saul asked the priest. "You gave David a sword."

"David is your servant," said the priest. "He is a leader. He is in your family. Everyone says he is an important person."

Saul turned to a shepherd. "Kill everyone who lives in Nob," said Saul.

One man got away and ran to tell David, who was hiding in a forest.

David felt awful. "Stay with me" he said. "Don't be afraid. Saul may want to kill you, but he wants to kill me, too. You're safe here." (1 Samuel 22:11-23)

Then David wrote this song. He used a word picture to help people understand. He said he is like an olive tree. To figure out what that word picture means, think of what an olive tree is like. Olive oil was used for food and medicine and fuel for lamplight. So olive trees were some of the most important of all trees. They grew well on rocky hillsides. Their roots spread out wide under the soil. As the tree grew older, it made more and more olives. Olive trees can live to be hundreds of years old.

So how is David like an olive tree? He lived in troubled, rocky times. His life grew up in God's care. As he grows older, more and more of his life showed God's love. Here is David's song about him and King Saul:

Psalm 52

Why do you brag about sin all day?
You are in sad shape.
Your words are sharp like a knife.
You trick people.
You love sin and not good.
You love lies and not the truth.
You love words that hurt.
I'm sure God will bring you down.
He won't let you live in peace.
God's people will see it.
They will be afraid.
They will laugh and say,
"Here is the man who did not trust God.
He trusted his riches.
He grew strong by hurting others!"
But I'm like an olive tree.
I grow strong in God's house.
I trust in God's love forever.
His love never ends.
I will praise him forever for what he has done.
I will trust in his good name.
I will cheer for him with all his people.

 Wednesday

Caves

There are lots of caves in the mountains and cliffs of Canaan. In David's time, some people lived in caves. Others used caves for places to bury the dead. Some people kept their sheep, cows, and donkeys in caves in winter or in stormy weather. When David ran from King Saul, he hid in a cave.
(1 Samuel 22:1)

David wrote this song when he was hiding in a cave. It sounds like he felt trapped there. Having to stay in the cave felt like being in jail to him. So this song is a prayer:

Psalm 142

I cry out loud to God.
I tell him my troubles.
My spirit gets weak inside me.
But you still know my way, God.
People have set a trap for me.
No one seems to care about me.
There is no safe place.
So I cry to you, God.
I say, "You are a place to be safe."
Listen to my cry.
I need you very badly.
Save me from those who chase me.
They are too strong for me.
Set me free from my jail so I can praise you.
Then people who do what's right will come around me.
They'll come because you are good to me.

 Thursday

Taking Grain from Barns

Long ago, when soldiers marched out to fight, only a few rode horses. Most soldiers walked wherever they went. They carried their armor and weapons with them. Sometimes a pack of donkeys or wagons went along to carry food for the soldiers. If anyone, like a captain, rode a horse, they had to carry food for the horses. Soldiers who were away from home a long time often ran out of food. Sometimes they would buy food from the towns they went to. Often they would just take food without paying. That may be what the enemy is doing in this story:

Someone told David, "The enemy is fighting in a town close by. They are taking grain from the barns."
David asked God, "Should we go fight the enemies?"
"Go ahead," said God. "Save the town."
But David's men said, "We're afraid."
So David asked God again. God said, "Go ahead. You'll win."
David took his men into town. They fought and won.
(1 Samuel 23:1-5)

Then David wrote these words:

Psalm 63

God, you are my God.
I look for you.
My soul is thirsty for you.
It's like being in a dry land where there is no water.
I have seen you in the worship place.
I saw your power and greatness.
Your love is better than life.
So my lips will praise you.
I will praise you as long as I live.
I will lift up my hands to show that your name is great.
My soul will be happy, the same way it is when I eat
 good food.
My mouth will praise you with songs.
I think of you when I go to bed at night.
You are my helper.
So I sing in the shadow of your wings.
My soul hugs you, and your right hand holds me.

 Friday

Oasis

Much of Canaan was desert, especially south and east of Jerusalem. There it was called the wilderness district. Land around the Salt Sea (also called the Dead Sea) was desert. Eastern caravans traveling to Canaan went around the south side of the sea and then up through the En-gedi Desert. They often stopped at an oasis there, where they found springs of water, vines and palm trees. The oasis there had the only natural waterfall in the land of Canaan. Important plants grew in En-gedi. Dates for eating, sweet-smelling plants used for perfumes, and plants used for medicines. When David ran from Saul, he hid in the En-gedi Desert. Here's the story.

Someone told Saul that David was in the En-gedi Desert. So Saul chased David there. He looked for David near the Rocks of the Wild Goats. There Saul and his men passed some sheep pens. Then they came to a cave. Saul had to go to the bathroom. So he went inside the cave. But it was the cave where David and his men were hiding. They were at the back of the cave.

David's men said, "God is giving your enemy to you today!"

David crept close to Saul and quietly cut off a piece of his robe. But then he felt bad about it. He said, "I shouldn't have done that to Saul. He is the king God chose." So David wouldn't let his men hurt Saul.

After Saul left the cave and went back to his men, David came out. He called, "My king!"

When Saul looked back, David bowed. "People say I want to hurt you," he said. "But why do you believe them? God gave me a chance to catch you today. In fact, some of my men told me to kill you. But I saved you. See? I cut off a piece of your robe. But I didn't kill you."

"Is that you, David?" Saul cried. "You're a better person than I am.

You were good to me. I hope God will pay you back with good things." Then Saul went back home, and David and his men went back to their cave. (1 Samuel 24) That's when, David wrote this song:

Psalm 57

>Be kind to me, God.
>I come to you for safety.
>I will be safe in the shadow of your wings
>   until trouble is gone.
>I call to God Most High.
>He saves me.
>He is mad at the ones who chase me.
>God sends his love.
>He keeps his promises.
>Lions are all around me.
>I lie down with hungry animals.
>They're really people who hurt other people.
>Their words hurt just as much as sharp swords.
>But you are great, God, above the sky.
>Shine your strong power over all the earth.
>My enemies put out a net to trap me.
>I was tired from being upset and sad.
>They dug a deep pit where I would walk.
>But they fell into it.
>My heart will stay with you, God.
>I will sing and make music.
>Wake up, my soul!
>Wake up, harp!
>I will wake up the day.

WEEK 2

 Monday

City Walls

Long ago, cities had walls around them to protect the people who lived in the city. Walls were usually made of clay mixed with reed. This clay was formed into bricks and baked hard in the sun. A city wall was built high and much thicker than walls of a house. Around the top of the wall was a walkway. The walkway on the walls of the city of Nineveh was so wide that three chariots could ride on it side by side. The walkway on the walls of Babylon were even wider. Six chariots could ride side by side around the top.

When an army attacked a walled city, the people in the city stood on the walkway and shot arrows at the soldiers below. So the soldiers closest to the wall were in the most danger. They were an easy target. They were in the hot spot. People said they were in the heat of battle.

In this story, Nathan says King David killed Uriah. But David didn't kill Uriah with his own hands. Instead, David told the captain to put Uriah in the hot spot at the front line of soldiers attacking a walled city. David knew Uriah would die there. That's the way David killed Uriah.

Then God sent the prophet Nathan to see David. Nathan told David that God said, "I chose you to be my people's king. I saved you from Saul. I gave you his kingdom. If that had not been enough, I would have given you more. So why have you done this terrible wrong? You killed Uriah."

David was sorry. "I've sinned against God," he said. (2 Sam. 12)

Then David wrote this song:

Psalm 51

Be kind to me, God.
Show me your love that never stops.
Erase my sins because you are so kind.
Wash away all my sin, and clean my heart.
I know my sins.
I always think about them.
You are the one who has really been hurt
    by this terrible sin.
I did wrong.
You are right when you say what's good and what's bad.
I know I was a sinner, even when I was a baby, even before
    I was born.
I know you want my heart to be true.
You teach me to be wise.
Clean me, and I will be clean again.
Wash me, and I will be whiter than snow.
Let me hear joy.
Let me be glad again.
Let my sad bones know joy again.
Hide your face from my sins.
Erase all my wrongs, and make my heart clean, God.
Put a spirit within me that stays true to you.
Don't send me away from you.
Don't take away your Holy Spirit.
Give me the joy that comes from knowing
    that you save me.
Give me a spirit that wants to follow you.
Then I will teach sinners your ways.

They will turn back to you.
Save me, God.
You are the God who saves me.
I will sing about how right you are.
God, open my lips, and my mouth will praise you.
I would bring a gift, but that's not what you want.
The gift you want is a heart that's sorry about
    doing wrong.
You won't turn away a sorry heart.

☐ Tuesday

Becoming a King

In long ago times, there were four ways a man could become a king. One way was to lead people to worship a fake god. People often thought this kind of king was a god. Egypt had this kind of king and queen.

A second way to become king was to be a leader in war. A war-leader took control with his army and ruled the people by force. A third way to become a king was to be chosen as a great man of your tribe or clan. A fourth way was to be the oldest son of a king. The oldest son would become king after his father died. King Saul hoped his son Jonathan would become king. But Jonathan died with King Saul, fighting in a battle. At that time, David was the war leader, and most of the people loved him. So they named him king. Not everyone loved David, though. This story is about someone in Saul's family who thought one of Saul's relatives should have become king.

This story happened when David and his army were traveling.

A man from Saul's family came out of his town and yelled bad things about David. He threw rocks at David and his guards. "Get out of here," called the man. "You're good for nothing!"

"Why let him talk to you like that?" an army leader asked David. "Let me take off his head!"

"You and I don't think alike," said David. "Maybe God told the man to say those things. Who am I to stop him?"

At last the king and his people got to where they were going. They were very tired, so they stopped to rest. (2 Samuel 16) That's when David wrote this song:

Psalm 3

Many people are against me, God.
They say, "God will not save him."
But you are like my guard.
You lift me up.
I call out loud to God,
and he answers me.
I can lie down and sleep.
I know I will wake up again
because God keeps me safe.
I will not be afraid,
even if ten thousand people are against me.
Come! Save me, God!

Wednesday

The Ark

The word "ark" means box or chest. When God wrote the Ten Commandments on stone, Moses made a special wooden box to put the stone in. God's people were traveling at the time, so they carried this ark with them. They called it the Ark of the Covenant, which means the box that holds God's agreement with them. Sometimes they just called it the Ark of God. Some people believed it was like God's throne on earth.

The ark was about the size of a rectangle shaped folding table or card table (two and a half feet wide, two and a half feet tall, four feet long). Nobody was allowed to touch it. Priests carried by holding poles that went through loops of metal on the long sides of the ark. The ark went wherever the Hebrews' place of worship was. In David's time, the ark was stolen by the enemy. When the enemy gave the ark back, it was kept in a house on a hill that belonged to a man named Abinadab. It stayed there until King David decided to move it to Jerusalem. This story tells about part of that move.

David talked to the army leaders. He said, "We didn't pray as we should have when Saul was king. So let's bring God's ark box back."

Everyone said this was a good idea. So David went to get the ark box. Many people went with him.

The leaders put God's ark into the tent David made for it. They offered gifts to God on the altar. David prayed for good things to come to the people. Then he gave each person a loaf of bread. He also gave each person a date cake and a raisin cake.

Then David talked to the priests who led the music. He told them to thank God with these songs: (2 Samuel 6:12-15, 17-19 and 1 Chronicles 15:13, 16:1-36)

Psalm 105:1-3; 96:1-8

Give thanks to God.
Call his name.
Tell the nations what he has done.
Sing praise to him.
Tell about the wonderful things he has done.
Enjoy his name. It's the best.
Let people who trust God show their joy.

Sing a new song to God.
Sing to God, all the earth.
Praise his name.
Every day, tell about how he saves.
Tell about the wonderful things he does.
God is great.
He should be praised more than anyone else.
The fake gods of the nations are only idols.
But our God made all of space.
Greatness and light are with him.
He is strong and powerful.
Tell how great his name is.

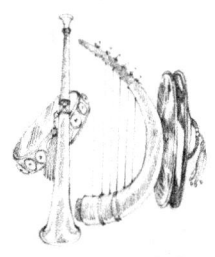

 Thursday

Tents

Tents of long ago were made with goat hair woven into strips. The strips were sewn together. So the tent had wide stripes of black and white. It took several people, often the women, to set up a tent. They hammered tent pegs into the ground. Then they tied several ropes to the tent and stretched them out to tie them to the tent pegs.

Inside the tent, poles about six feet high propped up the roof. Hooks on the poles made handy places to hang up things like cloaks or journey bags or pots for cooking. Sometimes mats or carpets were laid over the ground to make a floor covering. Other times, the floor was just bare dirt. Curtains or reed-cloth screens hung across the inside of the tent to separate it into rooms. One of the rooms was like a porch where people could sit and visit. The room behind the curtain was a storeroom and a room for the women. The only man who could go into this room was the head of the family.

As a shepherd and a soldier, David probably knew how to set up a tent. He probably slept in tents many times. He wrote this song after God saved him from all of his enemies. (2 Samuel 22) In this song, he calls the rain clouds God's tent:

Psalm 18

I love you, God.
You make me strong.
God is like a strong rock to me.
He is like a fort around me.
He saves me.
He is like my guard.
I pray to God.
I want to praise him.
When everything was going wrong, I asked God for help.
God heard me.
Earth's mountains shook.
God was angry.
Smoke and fire came from him.
God opened heaven and came down.
His feet stood on dark clouds.
He flew on the wings of the wind.
Darkness was his blanket around him.
Dark rain clouds were a tent for him.
But he was so bright that the clouds moved away
with hail and flashes of lightning.
God's voice sounded like loud thunder.
He made his enemies run by shooting lightning at them.
God's breath can open the way to the valleys in the sea.
God reached down and saved me.
When everything seemed lost, God helped me.
He was happy with me.
God, you keep my light shining.
You make dark turn into light for me.

God does nothing wrong.
What he says is right.
He watches over people who trust him.

 Friday

God's Angel

The word "angel" means "messenger." Most of the time, angels in the Bible bring messages from God to people. Sometimes the Bible talks about "the angel of God." We don't know exactly what that means. Maybe "God's angel" is one special angel who brings messages from God. Or maybe any angel who brings a message from God can be called "God's angel."

We do know that God sent his angel ahead of Abraham's servant to help him find a wife for Isaac. (Genesis 24:7) The angel of God spoke to Jacob in a dream one night. (Genesis 31:11) The angel of God traveled in front of the Hebrews to lead them out of Egypt and then stood behind them, between them and their enemies. (Exodus 14:19) The angel of God stood in the road to block Balaam and his donkey. (Numbers 22:22) So sometimes the angel of God seems to protect as well as bring messages. In this song, David says God's angel protects and helps God's people:

Psalm 34:1-10

I will always tell how wonderful God is.
My lips will always praise him.
My soul will tell how great God is.
Let everyone who has problems hear and be glad.
Praise God with me.
People shine with joy when they love God.
Their faces never look like they feel bad.
I called God, and he heard me.
God saved me from all my troubles.
God's angel stays around people who love God.
He saves them.
Taste and see. God is good.
Good things come to people who trust him.
People who love him have all they need.
Lions might get hungry and weak.
But people who look to God have every good thing
   they need.

WEEK 3

 Monday

School

If you lived in the time of King David, you would not go to school. Instead, you would be taught at home. Reading and writing and math were not the most important subjects to learn. In fact, many people, especially girls, never learned to read. Instead, children were taught to help with the work of their family. Boys would learn to tend the sheep, goats, and cattle, to plant and harvest crops, to hunt, to buy, sell, and trade. Girls, too, would learn to tend the animals. They would also learn how to spin yarn, weave cloth, and bake bread. All children learned about God.

We don't know who wrote this song, but it seems to be a song that parents used to teach their children.

Psalm 34:11-22

Come, my children, and listen to me.
I will teach you to love God.
If you want to love life, then don't say bad things.
If you want to have many good days, don't lie.
Turn away from sin. Do good.
Look for the way of peace.
God watches over people who do what's right.
God listens to them.
But God turns his face away from people who sin.
Nobody will remember them.
People who do right cry to God, and he hears.
He saves them from all their troubles.
God is near people who have broken hearts.
God saves people who are sad.
A person who does what's right might see lots of trouble.
But God saves him from all his troubles.
God takes care of him.
None of his bones will be broken.
Sin will kill bad people.
The enemies of God's people will not be saved.
But God saves his people.

 Tuesday

Shepherds

The rocky, rough hills and fields of Canaan made a good place for sheep and goats to graze. Sheep and goats were important to a family, because they were very useful. Goatskins were the water-bottles of David's time. Goat hair was woven into cloth for tents. Both goats and sheep gave milk for drinking and making cheese. Wool from sheep was spun and woven to make cloth.

Both boys and girls helped herd goats and sheep when the flocks were close to home. But the sheep and goats could not stay in one spot for long, because they would eat all the grass there and need to move around to find more. Then the boys and men would lead the sheep out to find fresh pasture.

David grew up taking care of his family's sheep. He protected the sheep from lions and bears. He always believed that it was God who helped him. (1 Samuel 17:34-37) David was the shepherd of his sheep, but he believed God was his shepherd. He wrote this song:

Psalm 23, by David

The Lord is my shepherd.
I am like his sheep.
I won't need anything.
He takes me to green fields
so I can lie down.
He brings me to quiet water.
He makes me strong again.
He leads me in the way that is right
because of who he is.
Sometimes I am in danger.
I'm like a sheep in a valley
full of shadows.
I may be in danger.
But I will not be afraid
because you are with me.
You make me feel safe.
You set a table for me
even when my enemies are around.
You make me feel special.
My cup flows over.
I have more than I need.
I know that love and good things
will be with me all my life.
I know I will live with God forever.

 Wednesday

Who Was Korah?

Some of the psalms in the Bible have a line at the top that tells when they were written. Sometimes a line tells what kind of music should go with the song or what tune it is to be sung to. And sometimes, a line tells who wrote the psalm. The writer was not always David. Some psalms were written by Korah's sons. Who was Korah?

The name "Korah" means "bald." Maybe Korah was a bald baby. We know he was a priest. And the sons of Korah were a well-known group of temple singers. Since they wrote many psalms, they may have collected their own songs together in one songbook, which would have made it one of the first hymnals.

One interesting fact is that this song-writer Korah was named after one of his great-great-great grandfathers who was killed in an earthquake. In this song, Korah's sons say that even if the earth shakes, they will not be afraid. Korah's earthquake story was probably still told at night around their campfires.

Psalm 46, by Korah's Family

God is like a safe place to be.
He is strong.
He is our helper when there is trouble.
So we will not be afraid.
Even if the earth shakes.
Even if the mountains fall into the sea.
Even if the oceans roar and make huge waves.
"Be still and know that I am God.
Nations will call me great.
The earth will call me great."
God has all power, and he is with us.

 Thursday

Rocky Places

Long ago in times of danger, people ran to high, rocky hills and mountains to be safe. From these high places, they could see their enemies coming. They could also fight them easier from above. People began building their towns and cities on hills and mountains. They hoped that would discourage their enemies from attacking. Because the high rocks were places of safety, God's people began to say that He was like a rock to them. In other words, God was their place of safety. He was the One who protected them. They sometimes called Him the Rock. In this song, David says, "Lead me to the rock that is higher than I am." He is talking about God.

Psalm 61, by David

Hear me call, God.
Listen to me pray.
I call to you from the ends of the earth.
I call to you when my heart gets tired.
Lead me to the rock that is higher than I am.
You are like a place where I can be safe.
You are like a strong tower.
I want to live with you forever.
I want to be safe under your wings.
Let the king live a long time.
May he rule and be near you forever.
Send your love to keep him safe.
And keep your promises to him.
Then I will sing praise to your name forever.
I will keep my promises to you every day.

 Friday

Forts

Long ago, safe places were often called "holds" or "strongholds." They were also called "fortresses" or "forts." (The word "fort" means "strong.") In the time of David, cities almost always had walls around them as protection from enemies. Inside the city walls, there might be a walled castle or walled towers, especially if a king lived there.

Forts in Canaan were often built in places that needed to be guarded. Some forts guarded major roads. Others protected passes in the mountains. And some were built on the border with other countries. Soldiers often lived in these fort cities. If enemy armies were coming, people who lived in the countryside near these forts would run to the fort and stay there for safety.

In this song, David says that God is like a fort to him:

Psalm 62, by David

I can rest only in God.
He is the one who saves me.
He is like a fort.
Nothing can shake me.
How long will sinful people fight?
They smile at lies.
They may say good things with their mouths.
But they say bad things in their hearts.
I trust in God.
He saves me.
He is like a fort.
Nothing can shake me.
I am safe with him.
Oh, people, always trust God.
Tell him everything in your hearts.
You are safe with God.

WEEK 4

 Monday

Hair

In the time of David, both men and women had long hair. Women sometimes braided their hair, but most of the time they wore it loose. Putting oil on someone's hair was a sign of great respect and honor. It became a custom to put oil on the head of someone who was chosen for a special job, like a priest or a king. Olive oil is the kind the Bible talks about most often. But they also used almond oil, cyprus oil, cedar oil, walnut oil, bay oil, and castor oil. They even used fish oil sometimes.

Gray hair or white hair was a sign of old age. If you lived in David's time, you respected people with gray or white hair. Older people were considered to be wise. You would be taught to honor them. In most families, grandparents taught their grandchildren about life. They told everyone the stories that had been handed down from their own grandparents. In this song, the writer asks God to remember him even when he is old and gray haired:

Psalm 71

I am safe with you, God.
Don't let me feel like nothing.
Listen to me and save me.
Be like a rock I can hide behind.
Save me from sinful people.
You alone are my hope, God.
I have trusted you since I was young.
I have counted on you since I was born.
I will praise you forever.

I talk about how great you are all day long.
My enemies talk about me.
They wait and plan to kill me.
They say, "God forgot him.
Let's chase him and catch him.
No one will save him."
Don't be far away, God.
Come fast to help me.
Get rid of my enemies.
But I will always have hope.
What you have done for me is more than I can measure.
You have been my teacher since I was young.
I still tell about the wonderful things you do.
Don't forget me when I am old, even when I have gray hair.
Let me tell children about your power.
You are right, God.
You have done great things.
Who is like you, God?
I have had many troubles.
But you will give me life again.
You will care about me.
I will praise you with the harp.
Because you keep your promises, God.
My lips will shout with joy
when I sing praise to you.
My voice will tell about
all the right things you do.

Tuesday

Who is Asaph?

King David chose a man named Asaph to play music at the worship tent until the temple could be built. Asaph's sons became musicians too. They served in the temple. Asaph was in charge of the singers, who sang every day. They often sang songs that David had given to Asaph. Sometimes the songs that Asaph and his singers sang in worship told about the mighty things God had done for His people. These songs helped people remember God's power and His goodness.

This song is by Asaph. Maybe his singers sang it. Or maybe it was a song he collected into a special song book. In this song, Asaph tells God, "Your path went through the sea." What event might he be talking about? (Hint: Think about Moses leading God's people out of Egypt.)

Psalm 77, by Asaph

I cried to God for help.
I looked for God when I was upset.
I held out my hands to him at night.
But my soul would not feel better.
I remembered you, God.

I thought about you, and my spirit felt helpless.
You kept me from closing my eyes.
I was too upset to talk.
I thought about the days that came before this.
I thought about years of long ago.
I remembered my songs in the night.
My heart thought.
My spirit asked, "Will God forget me forever?
Will he never show his love to me again?
Doesn't he keep his promises?
Does he forget to be kind?
Has his anger kept his kindness away?"
Then I thought,
"I will remind God of how he took care of us."
I will remember your wonders from long ago.
I will think of the great things you did.
Your ways are best, God.
You are the God who does wonders.
You saved your people with your strong arm.
The water saw you and splashed.
Clouds spilled their rain.
Your thunder was heard in the wind.
Your lightning lit up the world.
The earth shook.
Your path went through the sea.
But no one saw your footprints.

Wednesday

Sickness

Long ago, people did not know about germs. Many people did not know they should keep their houses, their cities, and their own bodies clean. So many people died of sicknesses that would be easy to heal today.

Some of the first doctors were in Egypt. Each of them studied a certain part of the body. One doctor would be good at healing eyes. Another would be good at helping stomach problems. Their medicines were usually herbs: leaves, flowers, and roots. Some doctors had special gardens to grow exactly the kinds of herbs they needed. Most medicines came from different parts of plants. Sometimes people used shells or bones that had been ground up. Sometimes they heated a bag of strong-smelling herbs and placed it on an infection. Olive oil was used as a medicine, and so was wine.

The Bible talks about doctors who lived in the time of David and even before David's time. They may have learned some of their ways of healing in Egypt. But there were probably very few doctors among the Hebrews. Most people probably lived their whole lives without ever going to a doctor. But in almost every town, there was a woman who helped when babies were born. Other people might know how to set a broken bone or mix herbs to help certain sickness.

In this song, the writer says God protects His people from dying of their sickness:

Psalm 91

The person who lives safe in God Most High
will rest in God's shadow.
God has all power.
I will talk about God.
I will say, "He is like a fort to me.
He is my God, and I trust him."
God will save you from traps.
He will save you from sickness that takes your life.
He will cover you with his feathers.
You will be safe under his wings.
His promises will guard you.
You will not be afraid of night.
You will not be afraid of danger in the day.
You will not be afraid of sickness.
A thousand people may fall down at your side.
Ten thousand may fall at your right hand.
But nothing bad will come near you.
You will only see it with your eyes.
You will see what happens to sinful people.
You can let God be like a safe house.
Live under his tent, and you won't be hurt.
Trouble will not come close to you.
God will tell his angels about you.
He will tell them to keep you safe.
They will lift you up in their hands.
You will not hit your foot on a stone.
God says, "I will save people who love me.
I will keep them safe because they trust in me.

They will call me, and I will answer.
I will be with them in trouble.
I will save them.
They will be important to me.
I will please them by giving them a long life.
I will show them how I save them."

Thursday

Afraid of the Sea

The whole west side of Canaan is the coast of an ocean that people long ago called the Great Sea. (Today, we call it the Mediterranean Sea.) But in David's time, the Hebrews did not like the sea. They had never liked the sea. They were desert people, happy with their sheep and donkeys and farms. It is true that some of them became fishermen. They built small boats and sailed on the Sea of Galilee. But the Sea of Galilee is really a lake, not an ocean. The Hebrew people never built large ships or sailed the Great Sea.

But their neighbors to the north, the Phoenicians (fo-nee-shuns), were famous sailors, well-known for boat-building. The Bible tells about their city of Tyre, which became a great seaport. So the people of Canaan sent their honey, oil, and wheat out on Phoenician ships to sell in other countries. Then they could buy the things the Phoenicians brought to Canaan from other places.

In this song, the writer says the sea belongs to God:

Psalm 95:1-7

Come!
Let's sing with joy to God!
Let's shout out loud to the one who saves us.
Let's come to him, giving thanks.
Let's worship him with music and song.
The Lord is our great God.
He is the great King above all gods.
The deep earth is in his hands.
The mountain peaks belong to him.
The sea is his. He made it.
His hands made the dry land.
Come!
Let's bow down in worship.
Let's bow before God our Maker.
He is our God.
We are the people of his field.
We are the sheep he takes care of.

 Friday

Alarm Clocks

In David's time, there were very few clocks. Some Hebrews may have measured time with an hour glass or water clock like people in Egypt used. An hour glass drips sand from one bowl into another. A water clock drips water. People could tell the time by looking at how much sand or water had dripped into the bowl.

Sun dials were also a common way to measure time. The sun's movement made shadows on the dial and showed people what time it was. But most people had no clock at all. They just watched where the sun was in the sky. The length of the shadows was also a good clue to tell time. The shorter a shadow is, the closer it is to noon.

But the sun is not an alarm clock. Hour glasses, water clocks, and sun dials don't ring. How did people know when to get up in the morning? Roosters would crow. Animals would begin to stir. And the sun would come up. Most people got up when the sky got light. They went to bed when it got dark.

In this song, David says he is going to wake up the morning. He plans to be up by sunrise, playing his harp and worshiping God.

Psalm 108, by David

My heart will stay with you, God.
I will sing.
I will make music with all my soul.
Wake up, harp!
I will wake up the morning.
I will praise you, God.
Your love is higher than the sky.
Be praised above the sky.
Show your greatness over all the earth.
Help us with your strong right hand.
Then the people you love will be saved.
God spoke from his home.
"I will measure out the land.
It is my helmet.
It is my washing bowl.
I toss my shoe on it.
I shout over it."
Help us win over our enemies.
People's help isn't good for anything.
We will win with God's help.
He will get rid of our enemies.

WEEK 5

 Monday

Hills and High Places

Hills run all the way through Canaan from the north to the south. Forts were often built on top of hills. But hills were also places where people who worshiped idols built their altars. These were called "high places." A high place would usually have an altar, a carving of a goddess, a large stone that stood for a god, and a building. Sometimes many idols stood at a high place. When God led the Hebrews into Canaan, He told them to get rid of these "high places." He meant that the people should get rid of the idols and altars on these hills.

Before the temple was built in Jerusalem, David worshiped God at a high place called Gibeon, where the worship tent was set up. This may have been the place known as "the hill of God."

In this song, the writer looks to the hills. But his help does not come from the hills. His help does not come from idols. His help does not come from forts built on the hills. Instead, his help comes from God.

Psalm 121

My eyes look up to the hills.
Where does my help come from?
My help comes from God.
He made heaven and earth.
God will not let you trip and fall.
He watches over you.
He never goes to sleep.
God is the shade at your right hand.
The sun won't hurt you in the daytime.
The moon won't hurt you at night.
God will keep you safe.
God will watch over you when you go out.
He will watch over you when you come in.
He will watch over you now and forever.

 Tuesday

Roads and Highways

If you lived in David's time, you would probably travel by walking wherever you needed to go, even to another town or city. The first roads were just paths that animals made by crossing hills and valleys over and over again. Animals' feet packed down the dirt and made a path that travelers followed. But these were not the best roads, so people began making roads. Still, these roads were dirt. So roads were muddy when it rained and bumpy when the weather was dry. When you came to a stream or a river, you would have to "ford" it. That means you rolled your carts and wagons across, and you walked or swam your animals across. The deeper the stream or river was, the more dangerous it was to ford.

Valleys could be marshy, and in the rainy season, water often rushed like a river through the valleys. So most roads stayed out of valleys and followed higher ground. Some roads in Canaan were as wide as ten feet, which would be enough for two lanes. Other roads were just paths, only wide enough to walk single-file.

There were plenty of bumpy, rocky roads and paths in Canaan. Those were not easy paths to travel. Even if you walked, it was easy to trip and fall on a bumpy path. This song is a prayer in which David asks God to lead him on smooth ground. That means he wants God to show him the right choices that will make his life go smoother.

Psalm 143, by David

Hear my prayer, God.
Help me because you do what is right.
You keep your promises.
Please don't judge me.
No one is as good as you.
The enemy chases me.
He pushes me to the ground.
So my spirit is not strong anymore.
My heart is afraid.
I hold my hands out to you.
My soul is thirsty for you.
Answer me quickly, God.
Don't hide your face.
If you do, I will be like a person who is lost.
When the morning comes,
   let me hear about your love that does not end.
Show me the way I should go.
Save me from my enemies.
You are a safe place where I can hide.
Teach me to do what you want,
   for you are my God.
I pray that your good Spirit
   will lead me on smooth ground.
Save my life, God,
   because of who you are.
Bring me out of this trouble,
   because you do what's right.
Your love never fails.

☐ Wednesday

Healthy Plants and Strong Pillars

David and the other writers of psalms often used word pictures to show what they meant. In this song, David says the sons of his people will be like healthy plants. The daughters will be like posts that make a palace pretty. These are word pictures. Healthy plants grow tall and strong. When they are full grown, they have fruit or berries, or they make shade. People enjoy them. Their seeds scatter and make more of the good and beautiful plants that the world needs. So David is saying that sons will grow tall and strong. They will become great young men. People will enjoy them. They will make the world a better place to live.

A post in a palace is called a pillar. Pillars support the roof and make a palace beautiful. They are strong. Even if the roof falls or the walls crumble, pillars are often the part of the building that is left standing. David is saying that the daughters will be strong and beautiful no matter what happens. They help hold up their world.

Psalm 144, by David

Praise God.
He teaches my hands to fight.
He is my loving God.
He saves me and guards me.
I go to him to be safe.
God, why should you care about people?
People are like a breath of air.
Their days are like shadows that fade.
Open the sky, God, and come down.
Touch the mountains and make them smoke.
Send flashes of lightning out.
Shoot your arrows and make your enemies run.
Reach down your hand and save me.
Save me from strangers who lie.
Then our young sons will be like healthy plants.
Our daughters will be beautiful,
   like posts that make a palace pretty.
We will have thousands of sheep in our fields.
Our oxen will be strong.
No one will break through our walls.
There will be no trouble in our streets.
Then the people will be happy.
Good things come to people
   when God is their Lord.

 Thursday

Rivers

If you lived long, long ago, when you traveled across dry, rocky land, you would watch for places ahead where there were trees. When you saw trees, you knew water was nearby. You needed that water to drink and wash. Sometimes people dug wells to get water for their towns. Other times, they built their towns near a lake or river.

Some rivers were used for travel. People rode barges or boats. They carried fruits, vegetables, and grains as well as things they had made to sell to people who lived farther down the river. They could also carry news and messages down the river with them.

The main river in Canaan was the Jordan River. It was never used much for travel. Instead, it became the east border of Canaan. The Jordan River kept the people on one side from the people on the other. Another important river was the Yarkon. After David's time, cedar logs were floated down the river into Canaan. The logs were then loaded onto wagons and taken to Jerusalem for building the temple. Not many people crossed the Yarkon River, because the land around it was swampy.

In this song, the writer says that people who follow God's way are like trees growing by the river. Trees by a river always have water to help them grow. People who follow God's way always have His wisdom to help them grow.

Psalm 1

Good things come to people
   who don't do what bad people tell them to do.
They don't follow sinful people.
They don't make fun of others.
They are happy to follow God's way.
Day and night they think about what God says.
They are like trees growing by the river.
They give fruit at the right time.
Their leaves never dry up.
Everything they do turns out good.
It's not this way for sinful people.
They are like dust that the wind blows away.
So they will not stand before God.
They will not be with good people.
God watches over people who do what's right.
But the path of sinful people will not last.

 Friday

Common Animals

If you lived in Canaan at the time of David, you would see many common animals. You would probably own some of them. You might have a donkey to ride or to carry packs or to pull a cart, wagon, or plow. Some people ate donkey meat, but the Hebrews didn't. They said donkey meat was unclean. You probably would not own a camel, but you would see them plodding along the trade roads in caravans. Camels would carry packs and people. You might have a tent made of camel hair, or even clothes made of camel hair.

You might own an ox or a bull. These were good work animals. You would probably have cows, sheep, and goats for milk and meat. Sheep provided wool for cloth, of course, and goatskin was used for tents. Most dogs ran wild, but you might have a small dog as a pet or a larger dog to herd your sheep. Horses were not used very often until the time of King David. His son Solomon built horse stables and used horses to pull chariots. You might see pigs, but you would not own them, because pigs were thought to be very unclean. You would never eat pig meat.

In this song, David says God cares for both people and animals:

Psalm 36, by David

Sinful people don't think God is important at all.
They are too proud to see their own sin.
Their words are lies.
They don't do what is wise or what is good.
Even when they lie in bed at night,
    they plan to do wrong things.
God, your love is as great as all of space.
Your promises reach up into the sky.
The right things you do are like strong mountains.
The way you are fair is like a deep sea.
God, you care for people and animals both.
Your love never ends.
It is greater than the greatest riches.
Some people are great. Some are not.
But all are safe in the shadow of your wings.
You have plenty in your house to feed them.
You let them drink from your wonderful rivers.
We see light because of your light.
Keep loving the people who love you.
Don't let proud people come against me.
Sinful people fall down.
They get thrown down, and they can't get up.

WEEK 6

 Monday

Common Plants

Lilies, wild crocus, rock roses, crown daisies. These are some of the flowers you would see if you lived in Canaan in David's time. Near the water, you might notice reeds with straight stems and feathery tops. If you were a writer, your pen might be made from a reed stem, which was like bamboo.

You would also see plenty of prickly weeds like thistles. But you would probably enjoy the fragrant flowers better. Cassia and cinnamon were used for perfume. White marjoram grew in rocky places. In bushy places, you might find rue with leaves that had a spicy-sharp smell. You might find myrtle, too, which had good-smelling leaves. For the Holiday of Tents, lots of people used myrtle branches to make tent-like huts to stay in.

Your mother might send you out to gather herbs to flavor her cooking. You might pick coriander leaves for a salad or use its spicy seeds to flavor other food. Cumin and dill also had spicy seeds. Mustard seeds were not only spicy but hot too. Mint leaves were good for a cooler flavor.

The most important grains you could grow were wheat and barley. Wheat would be ground to make flour. Barley grains could be roasted and eaten plain. If you were poor, it would probably be the only grain you would eat. Barley was also used as feed for horses and cattle.

Some of these plants would dry up after the growing season, though they would come back by themselves the next year. Other plants would die in cold weather. They would have to be planted by seed again the next year. In this song, David says people who do wrong are like these plants. After they have lived awhile, their lives seem to dry up or die out.

Psalm 37:1-11, by David

Don't worry because of sinful people.
Don't wish you were like people who do wrong.
They will dry up like grass.
They will die like green plants.
Trust in God, and do what's good.
Live and enjoy being safe.
Be glad in God.
Then he will give you
   what your heart really wants.
Choose to always follow God.
Trust him, and he will help you.
He will make the right things you do
   shine like the sunrise.
He will make your good ways
   shine like the sun at noon.
Be with God, and be still.
Be quiet and wait for him.
Don't worry when sinful people
   get away with doing wrong.
Keep away from anger, and don't worry.
It only leads to sin.
Sinful people will not get God's riches.
But people who trust God will get all God has for them.
Some day sinful people will be gone.
Even if you look for them, you will not find them.
But God's people will always have his riches.
They will enjoy peace.

 Tuesday

Pits and Marshes

When the Bible talks about a pit, it means a hole in the ground. The hole might be deep like a well or shallow like a ditch or marsh. In Canaan in David's time, there were lots of pits. Most of them were wells used to hold water for drinking, bathing, and cleaning. Water was so important that people sometimes fought over who owned a well. Or they might argue about who could get water from it. Sometimes the water in a well dried up. Then it might be muddy at the bottom. Or it might be totally dry. Then it could become a trap. A person or animal could fall in by accident. Or someone might throw another person in. That's what happened to Joseph. His brothers threw him into a dry well. They trapped him there.

In this song, David says his trouble was like a deep pit to him:

Psalm 40:1-10, by David

I was still, and I waited for God.
He heard my cry.
My trouble was deep like a pit.
He lifted me out.
He lifted me out of the mud.
He put my feet on a rock.
It was a strong place for me to stand.
God gave me a new song to praise him.
Lots of people will see this.
Then they will trust in God.
God will bring good things to people
   who trust in him.
Lord my God,
   you have done many wonderful things.
No one can even count
   the things you planned for us.
You didn't want me to bring you a gift.
Instead, you wanted me.
So I said, "Here I am.
There are words about me in your book.
I am happy to do what you want me to do, God.
Your way is in my heart."
I talk about how you keep your promises.
I talk about how you save me.
I don't hide your love and your truth.

 Wednesday

Riddles

Riddles are sayings that have hidden meanings. Here's a well-known riddle: She has a white dress and a red nose; the longer she stands, the shorter she grows.* The most famous Bible riddle is one that Samson made up after he killed a lion with his bare hands. He later passed by the lion's body. Only the bones were left. But bees had made a hive in the skeleton and had made honey there. Samson's riddle was: "Out of the eater, something to eat; out of the strong, something sweet" (Judges 14:14).

Sometimes a riddle is just a mystery, a puzzle, something we can't figure out. That seems to be the kind of riddle David talks about in this song. He says he will tell a riddle with his harp. Then he sings about the mystery or puzzle of riches. The puzzle is that some people spend their lives working hard to get rich. But in the end, they die like everyone else. They can't take their money with them.

Psalm 49, by Korah's Family

Listen, everybody.
I will tell a riddle with my harp.
Why should I be afraid of bad days?
Why should I be afraid of sinful people?
They trust in their riches.
No person can save another person.
No person can pay God to save him.
There is not enough money to buy a life.
Money can't help anyone live forever.
Wise and foolish men will all die.
They'll leave their riches behind.
People don't live here forever,
    even if they are rich.
This is what happens
    to people who trust in themselves.
They die just like sheep do.
Their graves will be far away
    from their big houses.
But God will save my life.
He will take me to be with him.
So don't be surprised when people get rich.
They won't take anything with them when they die.
People may say great things about them.
But when they die, it won't matter.

(*The answer to the riddle is: a candle.)

Thursday

Promises and Vows

A promise is saying you will do something. Or that you will not do something. The person to whom you make the promise can expect that you will do what you say. Sometimes we say someone "keeps his word." That means he does what he says. People can depend on the person who keeps his word. In the Bible, most promises are made by God. He promises to take care of those who follow Him.

A vow is kind of like a promise. One kind of vow makes a trade. It says, "If you do this, then I will do that." A vow to God might be like, "God, if you protect me, then I will pray to you three times a day." Jacob made that kind of vow (Genesis 28:20)

Another kind of vow is more like making a very important agreement with someone. It's an agreement that you mean to live by forever – or until a certain time. You plan never to break the agreement or go back on it. When people marry, they vow to stay together until one of them dies. In the Bible, some men made special vows to serve God. The most famous is Samson. As a sign of his vow, he never drank wine and never cut his hair.

In this song, Asaph writes as if God is speaking. God asks people to keep their promises to follow Him.

Psalm 50, by Asaph

God is the Strong One.
He is the Lord.
He calls the earth from the sunrise to the sunset.
God shines from his city, Zion.

Zion is a place that is good and beautiful.
God comes, and he is not quiet.
A fire goes before him.
A storm roars around him.
He calls heaven and earth.
He can see who is right and who is wrong.
He says, "Bring me the people
   who promised to be mine."
"Hear me, my people, and I'll speak.
I am your God.
I don't blame you for what you give me.
But I don't need bulls from your barns
   or goats from your pens.
Every forest animal is mine.
I own the cows on the hills.
I know every bird in the mountains.
The animals in the fields are mine.
If I were hungry, I would not tell you.
The world and everything in it is mine.
Give thanks to me.
Keep your promises to me.
Call on me when you are in trouble.
I will save you.
Then you will show how great I am."
But to sinful people God says,
"Why do you talk about my rules?
You hate my ways and don't obey my words.
You help robbers.
You go along with foolish people.
You use your mouths to say sinful things.
You use your voice to lie.
I have been quiet.
So you think I am just like you.
But if you forget God, no one will save you.
The people who give thanks show love for me.
They are getting ready for me to save them."

 Friday

Shoes

If you lived in David's time, you might go barefoot most of the time, especially if you were poor. Otherwise, you would wear sandals. Even in winter. The sole of your sandals might be made of a piece of animal hide the size of your foot. Or it might be made of wood or dry grass woven to fit your foot. A leather strap went through the sole of the sandal, then passed between your big toe and your second toe. Then the strap tied around your ankle. Sometimes people carried their shoes instead of wearing them. That made the shoes last longer.

Going barefoot or wearing sandals all the time meant that your feet always got dirty and dusty. So you would take off your sandals when you went into a house. You would take off your right sandal first, then the left. When you were ready to put them back on, you would put on the right sandal first, then the left.

In the song below, Asaph says his feet almost tripped. That's a word picture that means he almost made the wrong choice.

Psalm 73, by Asaph

It's true! God is good to his people.
He is good to people whose hearts are sinless.
But my feet almost tripped.
I nearly fell, because I wanted to be like the proud people.
I saw that sinful people get rich.
They seem to have no troubles.
They are healthy and strong.
They don't have problems like most people have.

So they wear pride like a gold band around their necks.
Their hearts are hard.
There is no end to their bad plans.
They make fun of people.
Their voices are full of hate.
They want to boss everyone around.
They say that heaven belongs to them.
They say the earth is theirs, too.
People who follow them believe what they say.
They say, "How could God know?"
That is what sinful people are like.
They don't have any cares.
They keep getting rich.
So have I kept my heart clean for nothing?
I've had trouble every morning.
I tried to understand this, but it was hard.
It was hard until I talked to God.
Then I knew what would happen to sinful people.
God, I know you put their feet
   on ground they can't stand up on.
You will tear them down all of a sudden.
You will wipe them away with fear.
You will stand up, God.
Then their good life will be just a dream.
But I'm always with you.
You hold my right hand, and you lead me.
Some day you will take me to greatness.
Who else do I have in heaven? Only you.
And all I want on earth is you.
My body and my heart may get sick.
But God makes my heart strong.
He is mine forever.
It's good to be near God.
That's where I go to be safe.
God, I will tell about the things you do.

WEEK 7

 Monday

Shields

If you were in the army in David's time, you would carry a shield. Some shields in those days were made of twigs or branches woven together. Other shields were made of leather. The woven branches or leather were stretched over a wood frame. A handle was on the inside. Sometimes soldiers would put flat "plates" of metal at different places on a leather shield so it would protect them better.

Shields were different shapes. If you carried a round shield, it would cover half of your body. It would be light and easy to carry. The rectangle shield was larger. It covered your whole body. It was so big that a shield bearer would have to carry it for you. Goliath had a shield bearer when he stood against David. (1 Samuel 17:41) If you didn't have a shield bearer, you could carry the rectangle shield in one hand and a long spear in the other. Archers would set these large rectangle shields in front of them, then shoot their arrows out from behind the shield.

Korah's family wrote this song. They said God is like a shield. He protects His people.

Psalm 84, by Korah's Family

The place where you live is beautiful, God!
My soul wants to be with you.
You are the living God.
Even the sparrow has a home with you.
  The swallow has a nest, too.
She can raise her baby birds at a place close to you.
You are the Lord Who Has All Power.
You are my King and my God.
Good things come to people who live in your house.
They always praise you.
Good things come to people who are strong in you.
They set their hearts on following you.
You make the valley flow with water.
Rain makes pools of water there.
One day in your house is better
  than a thousand days anywhere else.
I would rather be a door keeper in God's house
  than live with sinful people.
The Lord God is like a sun.
He is like a shield.
He makes people important.
He does not keep anything good
  from those who do what is right.
Good comes to people who trust you, God.

 Tuesday

A Very Old Song

In the psalms, along with songs from David and Asaph and Korah's family, there is a song written by Moses. It's a prayer song. For hundreds of years before it was written in the psalms, it was probably told or sung over camp fires. Just as we learn from reading David's prayers and songs, David learned from hearing and reading Moses' prayer-song.

Psalm 90, A Prayer That Moses Wrote

God, we have lived with you
    ever since you made people.
You were God before the mountains were born.
You were God before you made the earth.
Forever and ever you are God.
The way you see it,
    a thousand years are like a day.
They're like only part of a night.
People don't last long.
They are like the new morning grass.
It grows up in the morning,
    but by evening it's dry.
We are afraid of your anger.
You see our secret sins in your light.
We live 70 years, or 80 if we are strong.
But we see lots of trouble and sadness.
Our years pass fast, and then we fly away.
Teach us to use our years doing what's right.
Be kind to the people who serve you.
Every morning, fill us with your love that never ends.
Then we'll sing with joy as long as we live.
Make us glad for as many days as we have been sad.
Show our children how great you are.
Be kind to us.
Let good things come from the work we do.

 Wednesday

Music

Music was an important part of life for all Hebrews. If you lived in David's time, you could probably find a song to fit whatever you were doing. You might sing a song for bringing in the harvest or a song for digging a well. You might sing a song for baking bread or a song for weaving cloth. And of course, you would sing at times of celebration and at times of worship.

You might learn to play the lyre like David did. A lyre was like a small harp in the shape of a rectangle. Or you might play a harp, which was more of a triangle shape. Some harps were large enough to set on the ground. You might prefer to play the pipe, which was kind of like what we would call a clarinet or a recorder. Of course there were tambourines, cymbals, and rattles, too.

In this song, the writer talks about how good it is to play music for God:

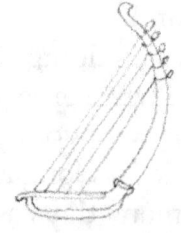

Psalm 92

It's good to praise God.
It's good to make music to your name, Most High God.
In the morning, it's good to tell
    about your love.
At night, it's good to tell
how you keep your promises.
It's good to make music on the harp.
You make me glad by what you do, God.
Your works are great,
    and your thoughts are deep.
Fools do not understand them.
Sinful people spring up like grass.
They may grow for a while.
But they will be torn down forever.
You are praised forever, God.
I know your enemies will die.
All sinful people will run away.
People who do what's right will grow like palm trees.
They will grow as tall as cedar trees.
They will grow in God's palace.
They will still grow fruit when they are old.
They will stay fresh and green.
They will say, "God is right.
There is no sin in him."

 Thursday

Trading, Buying, and Selling

Long ago, most family groups tried to make or grow whatever they needed. When you had more than your family needed, you would try to sell the extra to neighbors or take it to a market place in a town or city. If your family needed something you could not make or did not grow, you would trade for what someone else grew or made. You could trade in your own village with your neighbors. Or you could trade your goods to traveling salesmen called merchants. They would travel from village to village, buying and selling wherever they went. In a town, you would probably find the market place beside the town wall near the main gate. In big cities, the market might be a large open square where people set up booths to sell their goods.

There were other kinds of businesses, too. Men who knew how to write could be hired to write a letter or an agreement for you. There were potters and carpenters and metal workers, weavers and perfumers and tanners who made leather. In this song, the writer talks about how good it is when people are fair in their business:

Psalm 112

Praise God!
God brings good things to people who look up to Him.
They enjoy his commands.
Their children will be a success.
God brings good things to the families of people
 who do right.
Riches are in their houses.
Even in the dark, light will shine
 for people who do what's right.
They are kind and good.
They give to others. They are fair in business.
Those who do what's right will always be remembered.
They are not afraid of bad news.
Their hearts will keep on trusting God.
One day they will win over their enemies.
They give to poor people.
They will always do what's right.
They are strong.
Others treat them like important people.
Sinful people will see it.
They will be angry.
 Other people will forget them.
Their wishes will turn into nothing.

 Friday

Nations and Their "Gods"

In David's time, every nation claimed to have a different god. People thought that when two nations fought each other, the winner had the greatest god. So the losers would often give up their god and start believing in the god of the winners. Some nations believed in more than one god, and others believed in goddesses. They usually built figures of these gods and goddesses and worshiped these idols. People often thought that the god or goddess really lived inside the idol. Many times the idol stood in a building or temple. People thought the god lived in a temple like a king lived in a palace. Sometimes these idols were small enough to carry around, so that when they traveled, they could take their "god" with them.

The Hebrews were different. They believed that there was only one God. They believed He ruled over all the nations. He was real and could not be made small like an image. So they never made figures of what they thought God might look like. The Hebrews would not bow down to a figure made by human hands. This song is about the idols of other nations:

Psalm 115

You are great, God, not us.
It's because of your love. You keep your promises.
Why do nations say, "Where is their God?"
Our God is in heaven.
He does whatever he wants.
But their idols are made of silver and gold.
They are made by people's hands.
Idols have mouths, but they can't talk.
They have eyes, but they can't see.
They have ears, but they can't hear.
They have noses, but they can't smell.
They have hands, but they can't feel.
They have feet, but they can't walk.
They can't even make a sound.
People who make them will be like them.
People who trust in them will also be like them.
If you think God is the most important,
    you should trust him.
He is your helper and your guard.
God remembers us.
He will bring good things
    to everyone who looks up to him.
It doesn't matter if they are great or small.
The highest of all space is God's.
But he gave the earth to people.
We are the ones who praise God.
We cheer for him now and forever.
Praise God!

WEEK 8

 Monday

Wild Animals

If you lived in David's time, you would probably see wild animals now and then. But not in a zoo. You would see them in the hills and fields. You might hunt some of them, like deer. Smaller animals were probably fun to watch. Badgers dug their burrows in the ground, and coneys, which were like rabbits, would scramble around rocks. Bats would come out at night. Other wild animals were dangerous. There were hyenas, which were fox-like dogs, and jackals, which were dog-like foxes. There were also bears, lions, and boars, which are wild pigs. All of these animals could tear up vines and grain fields, and they could attack sheep, goats, and cows. Wild dogs were also a danger, especially when they ran together in packs. You would also probably see a snake once in awhile. Some were poisonous. They were called adders, asps, and vipers. Other snakes were not poisonous. You would also see geckos and lizards, frogs and tortoises. But they were not a danger.

In this song, David says God put people in charge of everything he made, even the wild animals:

Psalm 8, by David

Lord, our Lord, your name is great all over the earth!
Your greatness is higher than the sky.
You plan for children and babies to praise you.
Then your enemies are quiet.
I see the sky that you made with your hands.
I see the moon and stars that you put up there.
Then I wonder why you even think about people.
I wonder why you care about us.
But you made us only a little lower than
   the beings from heaven.
You made us important to you.
You put people in charge of everything you made.
They rule over sheep and cows and all the wild animals.
They rule over birds in the sky and fish in the sea.
Lord, our Lord,
   your name is great all over the earth!

Tuesday

Ships

Long, long ago, if you wanted to sail down a river, you might tie logs together to make a raft. But to cross the sea, you would need something better than a raft. So you might sew animal skins or leather onto frames made of tree branches. Some of the first boats looked like bowls. Others were square and made of tied bundles of reeds.

If you lived in Egypt, you might see long boats made of wood. About 50 men were needed to row each of these boats. Over time, people found out that they could put up a cloth sail and let the wind power the boat. They still used oars to row, though, when the wind was not strong enough. These ships carried mostly the goods that people wanted to buy and sell in faraway places. There were some ships, though, that carried soldiers to other lands to fight.

Most Hebrews never sailed on ships. They did not like the sea. But the man who wrote this song may have sailed on a stormy sea. He seems to know all about it.

Psalm 107:1-31

Give thanks to God. He is good.
His love lasts forever.
Let the people that God saved say so.
   He saved people from many lands.
Some people went here and there in the desert.
   They could not find a city to stay in.
They were hungry and thirsty.
Then they called to God, and he saved them.

He led them on a road that did not turn.
   He led them to a city where they could stay.
So let them thank God for his love that lasts forever.
Let them thank him for the wonderful things he does.
He gives thirsty people a drink.
   He fills hungry people with good things.
Some people sat in the dark.
   They were in jail with chains on.
They had not obeyed God.
   They did not think God was important.
So they had to work hard.
   When they fell, there was nobody to help them up.
Then they called to God, and he saved them.
He took them out of the dark.
   He broke off their chains.
So let them thank God for his love that lasts forever.
Let them thank him for the wonderful things he does.
He breaks down metal gates.
   He cuts through iron bars.
Other people sailed ships on the sea.
   They took loads of things to sell to other lands.
They saw the wonderful things God did in the deep sea.
God spoke and brought a storm.
   He made waves jump up high.
The ship tossed as high as the sky.
   Then it went down deep.
The people were in danger.
   Their boldness seemed to melt away.
They tripped and fell as if they were drunk.
Then they called to God, and he saved them.
He turned the storm into a whisper.
   He made the waves be quiet.
The people were glad when the sea was still.
   God took them to a safe place on land.
So let them thank God for his love that lasts forever.
Let them thank him for the wonderful things he has done.

Wednesday

Up in the Sky

In David's time, people said that what God created had three parts. The bottom was the earth, the middle was the sky, and the top was water. If you lived back then, you would call the sky "heaven." You would say that the sun, moon, and stars were in the heaven. You would also say that God stretched out the heavens like a tent and put windows in it so He could send rain through to the earth. You would say that lightning, frost, snow, and hail came also came through heaven's windows.

Many nations believed that stars were gods. They worshiped the stars. But the Hebrew people said God made the stars. Sun, moon, and stars show how great God is. So they didn't worship stars; they worshiped God. David wrote about it in this song:

Psalm 19, by David

The sky shows how great God is.
Every day it tells about God.
Every night it shows what he is like.
No matter what language people speak,
   they can understand what the sky tells.
All over the world, people can see it.
God has made the sky a tent for the sun.
The sun is like a groom getting married.
He comes out of his tent.
The sun is like a happy winner running a race.
It rises at one side of the sky
   and travels to the other side.
Nothing can hide from the heat of the sun.
God's way is the best.
It keeps us strong.
We can trust God's rules.
They make foolish people wise.
God's commands are right.
They fill our hearts with joy.
God's commands shine clearly,
   giving our spirits light.
God's rules are sure and right.
They are more special than gold.
They are sweeter than honey from the honeycomb.
Good comes to those who obey God's rules.
Keep me from choosing to sin.
Then I will do what's right and not what's wrong.
I want everything I say and think
   to make you happy, God.

 Thursday

Doorkeepers

In David's time, important buildings had doorkeepers. They stood at a door and said who could come in and go out. The king's palace had doorkeepers. So did the temple. Rich people might also have a doorkeeper. And a fort might have doorkeepers for some of its buildings.

A doorkeeper might be a servant or he might be a soldier. Sometimes doorkeepers were called gatekeepers, especially if they guarded city gates. The temple had gatekeepers too. Some of them guarded the money and other treasures stored at the temple.

In this song, David tells the gates and doors to open up for God, the great King. David's word picture may be a way of telling the gatekeepers and doorkeepers of the city to welcome God. We don't have city gates now. So when we read this song, we often think of how we are gatekeepers of our own hearts. We use this song to tell ourselves to open our hearts to God's love:

Psalm 24, by David

The earth and everything in it belong to God.
The world and everyone in it belong to him.
He made the land and set it on the sea.
Who can live with God?
Only people who don't have sin in their hearts.
   People who put God first.
God will send good things to them.
Lift up your heads, you gates.
Open up, you doors.
Then the Great King can come in.
Who is this Great King?
God! He is strong and full of power.
He is the Great King.

 Friday

Deserts

Deserts in Canaan were dry and rocky. The only rain that fell on the deserts of Canaan came in the spring. Then it would rain a lot. But it wouldn't last long. When it did rain, desert grasses and flowers bloomed. But most of the time, there was not much water there, so no one lived there. Most people did not even like to travel through deserts. If you had to travel through a desert, you tried to take a road that passed through an oasis. An oasis is a well or spring of water with some shade trees around it.

In this song, David talks about God's voice shaking the desert. David spent a lot of time in the desert when he was hiding from King Saul. Maybe in the desert he saw lightning and felt the earth shake like he says in this song.

Psalm 29, by David

Tell how great and strong God is.
Worship God.
Think of how beautiful he is, how special, how holy.
He is the best.
God's voice thunders over the sea.
His voice is great and full of power.
His voice is so strong, it breaks cedar trees in pieces.
His voice strikes like a flash of lightning.
It makes the desert shake.
It twists oak trees.
In God's house everyone calls out, "God is Great!"
God sits on his throne.
He is the King forever.
He makes his people strong and gives them peace.

WEEK 9

 Monday

Storehouses

Long ago, people built special houses for storing, or keeping, the grain they harvested or the wine and oil they made. These were called storehouses. Most storehouses were long, built in a rectangle shape. Big pillars went down the middle in two rows to make a main hall. On both sides of this hall were side rooms. That's where you would store your extra grain, wine, or oil. A small town might have one storehouse for everyone to share. A big city might have many storehouses. A rich farmer might build his own storehouse, just for himself. A king, too, would have his own storehouses.

In this song, the writer says God keeps the deep water in storehouses. Remember that people thought this storehouse was in the sky above the earth. (To read it again, go to page 82, "Up in the Sky.")

Psalm 33:1-11

Let those who do what's right sing with joy to God.
Praising God fits you.
Praise him with the harp.
Make music to him on the lyre that has 10 strings.
Sing a new song to God.
Play your best and shout with joy.
God's word is right and true.
You can trust him in all he does.
God loves what is right and good.
The earth is full of his love.
His love never comes to an end.
The sky was made by God's word.
The stars were made by breath from his mouth.
He brings the sea water together.
He keeps the deep water in store houses.
All the earth should be filled with wonder for God.
All people should know how special he is.
He said a word, and the world was made.
The plans of God's heart will always come true.

 Tuesday

Armies

Long ago, you had to know how to fight, because not everyone you met was friendly. Often, other people would come and try to take your wells. Or they might try to take your sheep and cows. Or they might try to chase you away from the land where you lived. So the first kind of army was the people in your family. If you met other friendly people, you might agree to be neighbors and live near each other. Then you and your neighbors could help each other if you had to fight unfriendly people.

After awhile, lots of people began to get together as nations led by kings. That's the way people lived in David's time. Nations would form an army of men whose job was to protect the land and fight away anyone who came to steal it. David was in King Saul's army. He was one of King Saul's best fighters.

But in this song, the writer says it's not big armies or strong fighters who save people. It's God.

Psalm 33:12-22

A nation can be happy when God is their Lord.
The people God chose can be happy.
These people are the ones God chose for his own.
God looks down from heaven and sees everyone.
He made their hearts,
  so he understands everything they do.
A big army does not save a king.
A fighter does not win just because he is strong.
A horse cannot save anyone, even if it's strong.
God watches over people who love him.
They trust him to give them what they need.
We wait for God.
He is our guard. He helps us.
Keep us in your love that never ends, God.
We trust you to bring us what is good.

Wednesday

Harvest

Grain was one of the most important crops that people grew in David's time. To plant grain seeds, you would first plow the ground. Most people had donkeys or oxen to pull sharp plows across the ground to break up the dirt clods. Then you would walk over the plowed ground with a bag of seeds. You would reach in, get a handful of seeds, and throw it across the dirt. Then you would hope for enough rain to water the seeds so they would grow.

When the grain was ready to pick or harvest, you would get your whole family out to help. You might even hire other people to help with the job. Or you might join with your neighbors. They would help you harvest, and you would help them. You would use a sharp curved knife called a sickle to cut the grain stalks. You would let poor people follow you to pick up the grain that you missed. You would let the keep whatever they found.

Other important crops were grapes and olives. A good harvest of any crop was something to celebrate. When the harvest was finished, there was a party. In this song, David talks about God bringing a good harvest:

Psalm 65, by David

God, we will keep our promises to you.
You hear us pray.
We were sad because of our sins, but you forgave us.
The people you choose are happy.
People everywhere hope in you, even those on the far seas.
People who live far away talk about your wonders.
You bring glad songs from the places where the sun
    rises and sets.
You take care of the land.
You water it and make it ready to grow crops.
Your rivers are full of water.
You soak the fields and make them flat.
You make dirt soft with rain.
You make good crops grow
    and give us plenty of food.
Carts spill over with more than we need.
The hills look glad, and sheep fill the fields.
Crops of grain cover the valleys.
They all shout and sing for joy.

Thursday

Prayer

People of other nations prayed to many different idols. Most of their prayers were asking for something. People often brought a gift to the idol when they prayed. They thought if they brought a gift, their god would do what they asked. If they needed rain, they would bring a gift and pray to the rain god. If they wanted a good harvest, they would bring a gift and pray to the god of harvest.

But the Hebrews prayed to only one God. Sometimes they let a priest pray to God for them. At other times, they prayed to God themselves. That's what David did. Other writers of the psalms did that too. Many of the psalms are their prayers. The writer of this psalm is very glad that God hears his prayer:

Psalm 66:16-20

Come and listen, if you love God.
Let me tell you what he did for me.
I called out to him.
I praised him.
If I had kept sin in my heart,
 God would not have listened.
But I know that God listened.
He heard me pray.
Cheer for God!
He did not turn away my prayer!
He did not keep his love away from me!

 Friday

Clothes

Everyone in Canaan and in most other countries wore tunics. That would be kind of like wearing a pillow case with a head hole and arm holes cut in it. Most people wore a long strip of cloth as a belt around their tunic. Tunics for men and boy often went only to their knees, though sometimes their tunics were longer. Women and girls wore tunics long enough to reach their ankles. Poor people had only one tunic to wear. It had to last through both summer and winter. But most people had two tunics, one for warm weather and one for cold. Only rich people had more than two.

Clothes were woven out of cotton or wool or goat hair or camel hair. Cloth called linen was made from a plant called flax. It was a lot of work to make linen thread from the flax plant, so linen cost a lot. Rich people wore clothes made of linen.

People liked colorful clothes, so they dyed the cloth. Red dye came from oak trees and some insects. Yellow dye came from almonds. Blue dye was made from a fruit called a pomegranate. Purple dye came from a kind of snail, and it was hard to make. So it cost a lot. Kings and queens might wear purple.

Everyone had to have a cloak, which was like a blanket you wore around your shoulders. It would keep you warm in cold weather. But it could also be a soft padded spot to sit on. Or it could be a blanket when you slept. If you were traveling and did not need to wear your cloak, you could fold it and carry things in it. Sometimes mothers carried their babies in a folded cloak.

In this song, the writer gives us a word picture. He says greatness is like the robe or cloak that God wears. Just as clothes are one of the first things we notice about people, greatness is one of the first things we notice about God.

Psalm 93

God is King!
Greatness is like a robe he wears.
He is strong.
The world stays where God put it.
It cannot be moved.
You became King long ago.
You have lived forever.
The seas lift up their voice.
The seas lift up their pounding waves.
God is stronger than the thunder of the waters.
God is stronger than the waves of the sea.

WEEK 10

 Monday

Judges

Long ago, old, wise men sat at the gates of their cities to visit and share news. They were the leaders of the cities. And they were the judges. People often came to these men to ask them to settle an argument or solve a problem. The old, wise judges would decide what was right and what was wrong. If they could not agree on what to do, they would send the people to a priest. Then the priest would be the judge. In the time of David, the king was the greatest judge of all. So if the men at the gate could not solve your problem, and the priest could not solve your problem, you would go to the king. The king would tell you what was right and what was wrong.

In this song, the writer calls God the Judge of the earth. He is the greatest judge. He knows what is right and what is wrong in every case.

Psalm 94:1-15

God, you are the one who pays sinful people back
   for what they do.
Stand up, Judge of the earth.
Pay the proud what they should get.
How long will sinful people be happy?
They brag and hurt your people, God.
They kill and say, "God doesn't care."
Listen, you fools!
When will you become wise?
God made your ears.
   So, of course, God hears.
God made your eyes.
   So, of course, God sees.
God is mad at the nations.
   So, of course, God pays people back for the wrong they do.
God teaches.
   So, of course, God knows everything.
He knows what people think.
People are happy when they obey you, God.
They are happy when you teach them your ways.
You save them from days of trouble.
God will not turn away from his people.
He will never leave his children.
He will say what's right and wrong.
All the people whose hearts are right will follow
   what he says.

Tuesday

The Poor

Long ago, you could become poor if you got too sick to work for your food and clothes. You could become poor if you borrowed money and could not pay it back. The person you owed might take everything you had. You could become poor if someone robbed you or took your land. If you were a woman and your husband died, you might become poor, because women could not get jobs. If you were a child and your parents died, you would become poor if no family came to help you. Or you could just be born poor.

In many nations, people thought you were poor because you were being paid back for something wrong you had done. Someone might give you a coin or something to eat, but they would not help you more than that. Poor people were thought to be bad people.

But the Hebrew nation was different. God told the Hebrews to take care of poor people and share with them. He told them to let poor people pick the leftover crops out of the fields. Sometimes a poor person let a rich person buy him. Then he would be a slave, working for the rich person without pay. But the rich person was supposed to take care of the slave, give him food and clothes, and treat him kindly.

In this song by David, he says he is poor. Maybe he wrote this song when he was running from King Saul. He was poor then. He had to ask people for food. Or maybe this is a word picture, a way for David to say he needs God.

Psalm 86, by David

Hear me, God, and answer me.
I'm poor, and I need you.
Keep my life safe, because I am all yours.
Be kind to me, God, for I call to you all day long.
Teach me your way, God.
I will follow you.
Give me a heart that is all yours.
Then I'll cheer for you, Lord my God.
I will praise you with all my heart.
I will always tell how great you are.
Your love for me is great.
You are a kind God.
You do not get angry quickly.
You have plenty of love.
You keep your promises.
Make me strong, and save me.
Give me a sign of your goodness, so that my enemies will see it.
Then they will not know which way to go.
You have helped me, God.
You cared about me.

 Wednesday

Horns

The first horns used for music were animal horns. They came from a ram or a wild ox. The ram's horn was called a shophar. It could play only two or three notes. It could be used to make music, but it was also used as a signal. A blast of a horn might mean danger. Or it might mean that somebody important died. Or it might mean a holiday was beginning.

Then someone had an idea. Why not make horns out of metal? So people began making horns out of silver. They were still shaped like animal horns, so they were still called horns. Trumpet is another name for this kind of horn. A trumpet call would tell people it was time to come to the worship house.

In this song, the writer is so excited about God's love that he tells everyone to sing and play their harps and horns:

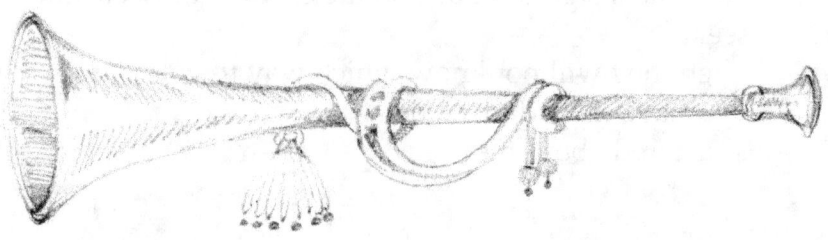

Psalm 98

Sing a new song to God.
He has done wonderful things.
His right hand saves.
He shows the nations how right he is.
He remembered his love.
He kept his promises to his people.
Shout to God with joy.
Sing happy songs with music.
Make music to God with the harp.
Make music with horns.
Shout with joy before God, the King!
Let the sea and everything in it shout.
Let the world and all who live in it sing.
Let rivers clap their hands.
Let mountains sing together with joy.
Let them sing to God.
He comes to judge the earth.
He will judge people by what is fair.

 Thursday

Zion

No one knows for sure what the word Zion meant before the time of David. Some people think it meant "dry place." Others say it meant "top of the hill." People used the word Zion when they were talking about a fort that sat on a hill between two valleys. The real name of the fort was Jebus. David led his men to fight the people who held that fort, and David won the fight. He moved into the city. So people started calling it the City of David. Later that city became Jerusalem. The writers of the psalms often call Jerusalem "Zion," as in this song:

Psalm 99:1-5

God is the King.
He sits in the King's chair between the heavenly beings.
Let the earth shake!
God is great in his city of Zion.
He is great over all the nations.
Let them praise his great and wonderful name.
God is holy. He does no wrong.
The King is strong.
He loves what's fair and right.
Treat God as the most important one.
Worship at his feet, for he is holy.
The Lord our God never does wrong.

 Friday

Palaces

In David's time, most houses were small and made of mud brick. Some had only one or two rooms. Even if your house had more rooms, each room was small. People spent much of their time outdoors. Even cooking was done outside. So people must have been amazed when they looked at a palace where the king lived. A palace was the biggest building around.

Kings wanted to show how rich and powerful they were. Their palaces were built to amaze people. The Bible tells us that King David's palace was built with stone and cedar wood. Cedar wood has a nice, spice-wood smell, so it would make the palace smell good. Many palaces had pillars and beautiful curtains and tiled floors and carpets. In a palace, there were lots of rooms. There were storerooms and dining rooms, libraries and kitchens. There were also bedrooms for family and servants. In ordinary houses, people slept on mats on the floor. But in a palace, there would be beds with pillows and blankets. There would be fine wooden furniture. It might be carved or have small tiles glued into the wood in fancy designs.

In this song, the writer says to go into God's palace with praise. He is probably talking about the temple, which was built by David's son Solomon. In many ways, the temple looked like a palace. It was very large and very beautiful.

Psalm 100

Let all the earth shout to God with joy.
Worship God and be glad.
Come to him with songs of joy.
Know that the Lord is God.
He made us.
We are his people.
We are like sheep from his field.
Go through God's gates giving thanks.
Go into his palace with praise.
Give thanks to him.
Cheer for his name, because God is good.
His love lasts forever.
He always keeps his promises.

WEEK 11

 Monday

Clans

A clan is a large family group. Your clan is your father and mother, sisters and brothers, aunts, uncles, grandparents, and even great-grandparents. Long, long ago all the people in one clan lived together. They helped each other work and play. They traveled together and built together and dug wells together. Even servants who worked for your family were sometimes listed as part of your family. Sometimes even animals were considered part of your family!

In a clan, your cousins might be as close to you as your brothers and sisters. Even though your mother loved you in a special way, your grandmothers and your aunts might also seem like mothers to you. If you were a girl in the clan, your mother and aunts and grandmothers would help you and teach you how to become a woman.

The oldest man in the clan was treated as the "father" of the family even though he may have been your grandfather or great-grandfather. He was the one in charge of everyone and everything. Your own father and uncles would talk about news and work and problems with him. If you were a boy in the clan, your father and uncles would help you and teach you to be a man. The family was sometimes called the "father's house."

In this song, David says God is a kind, loving father. He is good to his children's children.

Psalm 103, by David

I say to my soul, "Cheer for God!"
Everything in me, praise his holy name!
Don't forget the good things he has done.
He forgives all your sins.
He makes you well from every sickness.
He saves your life.
He is loving and kind to you.
He answers your wishes with good things.
When you grow old, you feel young again.
You feel strong, like the eagle.
God does what is right and fair.
He is full of love and kindness.
He does not get angry quickly.
Love flows out of him.
He won't always blame us.
He won't be angry forever.
He doesn't pay us back for our sins,
    even though that's what should happen.
God's love is as high
    as the sky is above the earth.
He has moved our sins away from us
as far as the east is from the west.
God is loving and kind to people who worship him.
He is like a father
    who is loving and kind to his children.
He remembers that we're made out of dust.
His love is always with people who worship him.
He is good to their children's children.
Cheer for God, you angels.
You are the strong ones who do what he says.
Cheer for God, everything everywhere in his kingdom.

 Tuesday

Winds

In Canaan, rain and storms often came with a wind that blew from the mountains and the sea in the west. Dry winds blew from the deserts in the south and east and could dry up the plants. There were breezes and storm winds and whirlwinds. Because all these winds came from different directions, people said that winds came from the four corners of the earth.

Wind often made people think about God. They said only God can tell the wind what to do and how to blow. Sometimes people called the wind God's breath. They said that with His breath, God could freeze rivers. (That would be a cold wind.) Or with His breath, God could make the grass dry up. (That would be a hot wind.)

In this song, the writer says that God rides on wings of wind and that winds take His messages:

Psalm 104:1-16

Cheer for God, my soul!
The Lord my God is very great.
Wonder and greatness are like clothes on him.
He wraps himself in light.
He rolls out the sky like a tent.
He puts his upstairs rooms in the rain clouds.
He makes his chariot from clouds.
He rides on wings of wind.
Winds take his messages.
Flames of fire serve him.
God put the earth where he wanted it.
It can never be moved.
The waters were above the mountains.
But they rushed away when they heard his thunder.
They flowed over the mountains into valleys.
They went where God told them to go.
He drew a line they cannot cross.
They will never cover the earth again.
God makes springs of water flow into rivers.
They give water to all the animals in the field.
Wild donkeys drink.
Birds make nests by the water.
They sing in the tree branches.
God waters mountains from his upstairs rooms.
He makes grass grow for cows.
He makes plants grow for people to use.
Food comes up from the earth.
   Then people can make wine and oil.
   People can make bread so they'll be strong.
God's trees have plenty of water.

Wednesday

A Moon Calendar

Long ago, the Hebrews measured their year by watching the sky. They saw how the moon changed its shape. The moon starts out looking like a backwards C. As the month goes by, it looks larger and larger. That means we see more and more of it until it looks like a round circle, a full moon. Then we see less and less of it until it looks like a C. Then it gets dark. After that, it starts all over again as a backwards C. The time when it is dark is called the "new moon." Every new moon was the beginning of a new month for the Hebrews. The priests watched the sky and blew their trumpets for the time of the new moon, the beginning of a new month.

The Hebrew people started their new year in the fall after the harvest. They usually just numbered the months from one to twelve. So they would say, "You were born in the fourth month." Or "We moved to this land in the second month." But some Hebrews called the months by the names the people of Canaan used. We know only a few of those names. March was Abib. April and May were Ziv. September was Ethanim. October and November were Bul.

In this psalm, the writer says the moon shows the seasons:

Psalm 104:17-35

The stork makes its home in the pine trees.
Wild goats live in the high mountains.
Badgers hide in the rocks.
The moon shows the seasons.
The sun knows when to go down.
God brings the darkness.

Then forest animals come out to look around.
Lions roar for food.
They look for the food God gives them.
When the sun comes up, they creep away.
They go back to their dens and lie down.
That's when people go off to work.
They work until evening.
You have made so many things, God!
You made them all by your wisdom.
The earth and the deep, wide sea
   are full of living things you made.
There are too many to count.
There are all kinds of living things.
Some are big, and some are small.
They all look to you, God.
They look for food from you
   when it's time to eat.
You open your hand and give it to them.
Then they are full.
But when you hide your face,
   they are afraid.
When you take their breath away,
   they die and turn into dust again.
When you send your Spirit,
   new life begins.
You make things on the earth new.
May God's greatness last forever.
May God show his joy
   when he sees what he has made.
He looks at the earth, and it shakes.
He touches mountains, and they smoke.
I will sing to God all my life.
Cheer for God, my soul!
Praise God!

Thursday

Servants and Slaves

Servants worked for other people. Sometimes they got paid. Most of the time they did not. Instead, they lived with the family they worked for. Many servants were slaves. That means the family bought them and owned them. You might become a slave if you were captured in a war. Or if your parents could not take care of you, they might sell you to someone. Or you might be born to a mother and father who were already slaves. Sometimes people who had stolen or killed were punished by being sold as slaves. Or if you did not have enough money to buy food, you might sell yourself to a family. You would work for them and they would feed you and give you clothes and a place to live.

Servants and slaves were not just from one people group. They could come from any country. The people who bought and owned the slaves were called their masters. A master could be mean or a master could be good. The Hebrews were supposed to be good masters and treat slaves kindly. Slaves were often considered part of the family.

In this song, the writer talks about being servants of God. God is the best master. Being a servant of God is like being part of His family.

Psalm 113

Praise God!
You servants of God, cheer for his name.
Praise his name now and forever.
His name should be praised from sunrise to sunset.
God is great over all nations.
His power is great above the sky.
Who is like God?
He sits on the King's chair in heaven.
He bends down to look at the sky and the earth.
God helps poor people.
He takes them to sit with princes.
He gives children to the woman who thought
   she would never have any.
He makes her happy in her home.
Praise God!

 Friday

The Law

In David's time, when people talked about the Law, they were talking about the story of God from the time He made the earth to the time He gave Moses rules about how to live. All fathers were supposed to teach these things to their children. All children were supposed to learn and obey them. It was all a part of being a Hebrew. The Hebrew people saw the law as a gift from God to them. The Law helped them know how to be healthy and happy. It helped them know how to treat others so everyone they met could be healthy and happy too. In this song, the writer tells how important the Law is to him:

Psalm 119:1-16

Good things come to people who do what's right.
They keep God's rules. They obey him.
They look for God with all their hearts.
They don't do wrong.
You have told us your rules, God.
We should obey all of them.
I wish I would always do what you want me to do.
Then I would never feel bad.
I will praise you with a heart that's right.
How can a young person keep doing what's right?
By following your word, God.
I look for you with all my heart.
Don't let me turn away from your law.
I have hidden your word in my heart
  so I won't sin against you.
I'm glad to follow your rules.
I will not forget your word.

WEEK 12

 Monday

Money

Long, long ago, people had no money. They traded what they had for something someone else had. This was called barter. Then they found that different kinds of metal could be traded. Silver and gold and copper were very good for trading. So they traded bars of these metals as well as gold and silver bracelets and necklaces, plates and cups. It was very important to weigh these metal objects, because how much they weighed showed how much you could buy. If the metal weighed a lot, you could buy more. If it weighed a little, you could buy only a little.

Trading was still the way to buy and sell in the time of King David. They did not have coins yet. In this song, the writer talks about God's law being more special to him than a thousand pieces of silver or gold. He is probably not talking about coins, but about small bars or jewelry.

Psalm 119:65-72

Do good to me just like you said, God.
Teach me what I need to know.
Teach me to choose wisely.
I believe in your rules.
In the past I did what was wrong, but now I obey you.
You are good, and what you do is good.
Proud people lie about me.
Their hearts are hard.
They have no feelings.
But I keep your laws with all my heart.
It was good for me to have trouble,
    because I learned your rules.
Your law is more special to me
    than thousands of pieces of silver.
It is more special to me
    than thousands of pieces of gold.

 Tuesday

Eyes

The Hebrews treated eyes as a very important part of the body. If a master hit a slave in the face and it made him lose sight in his eyes, then the master had to let the slave go free. If you could not see, you could not be a priest, helping people worship God.

But they also used eyes as a word picture. They said your eyes could be greedy or unhappy. Or your eyes could agree with someone. The "light of your eyes" meant being strong. So when people said God's rules could give light to your eyes, they meant that God's rules could make you strong. In this song, the writer says his eyes are foggy. That probably means he is not sure about what is going to happen.

Psalm 119:81-96

My soul gets weak,
    because I want so much for you to save me.
My eyes are foggy,
    because I have looked so long for your promise.
I say, "When will you cheer me up?"
I feel like I'm in a cloud of smoke.
But I don't forget your rules.
How long do I have to wait?
When will you pay people back for doing wrong?
Proud people try to make me fall.
Help me.
People are mean to me for no reason.
They almost got rid of me.
But I didn't turn away from your rules.
Save my life by your love.
Then I will obey you.
Your word and your promises last forever, God.
I am happy with your law.
If I had not been,
    I would have died in my trouble.
I will never forget your commands,
    because you saved my life.
Sinful people wait to get rid of me.
But I will think about your rules.
Even the best things go only so far.
But your rules last forever.

 Wednesday

Lamps

In the time of David, lamps were always made out of clay. We would call them pottery lamps. They were shaped like an open bowl that had a spout. A thin twisted cord of flax, called a wick, lay in this spout. Part of the wick stuck out and part of it went into the bowl. Oil was poured into the bowl and the wick soaked it up. You would light the end of the wick that stuck out of the bowl so the wick would burn and make light for you.

For a light outdoors, you would use a torch. Torches were long poles with cloths wrapped around the end. The cloth end was dipped in oil and then lit. The oil they used for lamps and torches was mostly olive oil. But sometimes they used oil from nuts or fish.

In this song, the writer uses a lamp as a word picture. He says that God's word is like a lamp, a light for his path. That means that God's word helps him know how to live and what choices to make.

Psalm 119:97-112

I love your law so much!
I think about it all day.
Your rules make me wiser than my enemies.
I understand more than my teachers do.
I understand more than the leaders do.
That's because I think about your rules.
I stay away from sin.
Your words taste so sweet!
They are sweeter than honey in my mouth.
Your commands teach me to understand.
So I hate everything that is wrong.
Your word is like a lamp
    that shows my feet where to go.
It is like a light for my path.
I may put my life in danger.
But I won't forget your law.
Sinful people set traps for me.
But I will not leave your ways.
Your rules will be my gift forever.
They fill my heart with joy.

 Thursday

Guards

Long, long ago, when people lived in clans and tribes, every man learned how to fight. That meant you had to learn how to use at least one kind of weapon. Most men knew how to use many different kinds. There were clubs and axes, long swords and short swords. There were darts and spears and javelins to throw. There were bows and arrows and even slings for throwing stones. You would practice with these weapons. It was like a game to see who could hit the target or throw the farthest.

But a real fight was not a game. So you would use some of your soldiers as guards, even if you didn't think there was an enemy nearby. Because enemies liked to surprise the people they were going to fight. They had a better chance of winning if they attacked when they were not expected. So guards would stand at places where they could see what was going on around them. They would watch for danger. Sometimes they were called "the watch." You could sleep easier at night because you knew the guards would wake you up if danger came.

A king's guards were sometimes called runners, because they ran beside the king's chariot. They were there to watch for danger and protect the king. In this song, the writer says that God is his guard:

Psalm 119:113-128

I hate people who say one thing
    and then say a different thing.
They can't make up their minds.
But I love your law.
I can go to you to be safe.
You are my guard.
The words you say give me hope.
Get away from me, you sinful people.
I want to obey God!
Hold me, God. Then I'll be safe.
I will always follow your rules.
You are so great!
I shake when I think about it.
I wonder at your laws.
I have done what is right and fair.
Don't leave me alone with my enemies.
Make sure I'm all right.
Don't let proud people boss me around.
Show me your love.
Teach me your rules.
It's time for you to do something, God.
People are not obeying your law.
I love your law more than gold.
I know that all your commands are right.

 Friday

Beds and Blankets

Long ago, many people slept on mats that they rolled out on the floor at night. In the daytime, they would roll up their mats, because they needed room to work. If you were very poor, you might have a thin mat stuffed with straw or a cloth pad with no pillow. If you were traveling, you might have only your cloak to lay on at night. You would probably try to roll it around you to keep warm. You would have no pillow. When Jacob traveled, he used a stone as a pillow. (Genesis 28:10-11) That was not really so strange. In Egypt, even the kings and rich people used special neck rests carved out of stone.

Rich people had larger houses with bedrooms. Their beds were raised off the floor. Some bed frames were made of wood. Some were metal or stone. Some of the richer people had beds carved out of ivory, which comes from an elephant's trunk.

In this song, the writer talks about singing in bed:

Psalm 149:1-5, 9

Cheer for God!
Sing a new song to God.
  Sing praise to him together with everyone
    who loves him.
Let God's people show joy in their Maker.
  Let them praise him with dancing.
Let them make music to him with the tambourine
  and the harp.
God is happy with his people.
  He saves them.
So let them show their joy and sing with joy in bed.
Praise God!

WEEK 13

 Monday

Rocks and Stones

The land of Canaan was very rocky. If people wanted to plant fields for farming, they first had to clear away the rocks. They found lots of ways to use rocks and stones. Sometimes they used rocks and stones as weapons. David fought Goliath by throwing stones at him. People sometimes hurt their enemy by scattering rocks on his field so he would have a hard time growing his plants. Other times, they blocked up the enemy's wells with rocks so he couldn't get water.

But they found good ways to use rocks and stones too. They built city walls and houses with large stones. A big stone could be a cover for a well, or it could be a marker to show where your land ended and your neighbor's land began. Some people wrote on stones. After something special happened, people might heap up a pile of stones to help them remember the event. People also stacked stones to make altars used for worship. They built fires on these altars and brought gifts and prayed there. Sometimes an altar was made out of one giant stone.

When stone masons were building walls and houses, they placed a special stone at the corner to hold two walls together. This stone was called the cornerstone. The cornerstone made the wall stronger. In this song, the writer tells about a stone the builders didn't want. But that stone became the cornerstone. We call this kind of song a "prophetic" song, because it tells what is going to happen. This song told about Jesus long before He was born. Jesus is like that stone. Most of His people did not want Him. But He became the one who holds all of life and love.

Psalm 118:1, 5-6, 8-16, 19-24, 28-29

Give thanks to God. He is good.
> His love lasts forever.

While I was upset, I called to God.
> He answered me and set me free.

God is with me.
I will not be afraid.
> What can people do to me?

It is better to trust in God than to trust in people.
All the nations came to fight me.
> But I won in God's name.

They were like bees around me.
> But they burned out like weeds on fire.

They pushed me back, and I almost fell.
> But God helped me.

God makes me strong.
> He saves me.

Shouts of joy come from the tents of people
who do what is right.
They say, "God's right hand has done powerful things!"
Open the gates to what's right.
> I will go in and give thanks to God.

People who do what is right may go in.
I will thank you, God, because you answered me.
> You saved me.

There was a stone that builders didn't want.
> Now that stone holds up the whole building.

God made this happen.
> We think it's wonderful.

This is the day that God has made.
> Let's show our joy and be glad today.

You are my God.
> I will thank you.
> I will treat you as the most important one.

Give thanks to God. He is good.
His love lasts forever.

 Tuesday

Towers

Long ago, towers were built so that guards or watchmen could look out and watch for danger. So towers had to be tall. Most towers were built of stone, but some were made of wood.

Sometimes towers were in fields where cows and sheep would go. Sometimes they were in fields of crops, like the places where grape vines grew. These towers might be tall, but not very wide. Guards in these towers would watch for robbers and wild animals.

Sometimes towers were in cities and forts. These towers were tall and wide, too. In fact a whole fort could be a tower. Guards in these towers would watch for enemies and other people who might cause trouble.

In times of trouble, people might run into the tower to stay safe. In this song, David prays for safety around the towers of Jerusalem:

Psalm 122, by David

I was glad with the people who said,
"Let's go to God's house."
Our feet stand at your gate, Jerusalem.
Jerusalem is a city with buildings close together.
That's where God's people go.
They go there to praise God's name.
That's where the judges sit.
Pray for Jerusalem to have peace.
"I pray that people who love you will be safe.
I pray that there will be peace in your city.
I pray that there will be safety around your towers."
Then my family and friends will be safe.
I will pray for good things to come to Jerusalem.

 Wednesday

Snares and Traps

Long ago, hunters often used snares and traps to catch animals. One kind of snare was just a rope or cord. If the hunter placed the rope in a circle on the ground, when the animal stepped into it, the hunter pulled it tight to catch the animal. If the hunter held the rope from above, he could drop it over the animal's neck and pull it tight.

Another kind of snare is a net. The hunter spread out the net. On top of it, he placed something the animal liked. That was called the bait. The animal would come to get the bait, and the net would spring up around the animal to catch it.

Another kind of trap was a pit dug into the ground. The hunter might put the bait in the bottom. Then he would cover the pit with sticks and leaves. An animal would be too heavy for the sticks and leaves to hold him up. So when the animal stepped on the sticks and leaves, he would fall into the pit.

In this song, David talks about how God helped him get away from his enemy. He says he and his friends got away like a bird getting out of a trap.

Psalm 124, by David

Men came to fight us.
They were angry with us.
God was on our side,
 or they would have eaten us alive.
Our troubles would have covered us like deep water.
They would have taken us away.
Praise God.
He did not let them get us.
We got away like a bird gets out of the hunter's trap.
The trap broke, and we got away.
Our help is in God's name.
He is the Maker of heaven and earth.

 Thursday

The Worship House

The first worship house the Hebrews had was a tent. God told Moses how to build this tent. The Hebrews took the worship tent with them wherever they traveled and set it up in the middle of their camps. All their other tents would be set up around the worship tent. People would bring gifts for God to the worship tent, but only priests could go inside.

After the Hebrews moved to Canaan to stay, they set up this tent at a place called Shiloh. That's where it was when David was growing up. After David became king, he wanted to build a worship house, a temple, for God in Jerusalem. But God told David that his son Solomon would be the one to build the temple. Still, David made the plans for building it.

In this song, David says he will bow down toward the worship house. He may be talking about the worship tent. But he was probably talking about the worship house he was planning, the one Solomon would one day build.

Psalm 138, by David

I will praise you, God, with all my heart.
I will sing your praise.
I will bow down toward your worship house.
I praise you for your love.
I praise you for keeping your promises.
You made your name and your word to be the greatest.
You answered me when I called.
You made me bold and gave me a brave heart.
I may have trouble.
But you save my life, God.
You hold out your hand to stop my angry enemies.
God will do what he planned for me.
God, your love lasts forever.

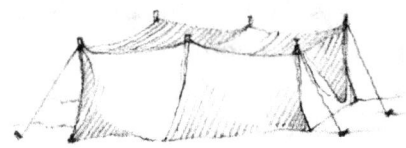

☐ Friday

Books

In the time of David, there were no books like we have. Instead, there were tablets and scrolls. Most people could not read or write. If you needed something written, you would hire a scribe to write it for you. Kings had scribes and so did traders. When someone sent a message on a tablet or scroll, a reader would read it aloud to the people who could not read.

The first writing was done on large flat stones called tablets. To write on stone, you would use a small sharp tool called a chisel. You would hammer the chisel on the stone until it dug out the right shape for the word or sound you were writing. Then someone had the idea of making tablets out of clay. It was easier to write on than stone. You would use a stick called a stylus to mark letters into the soft clay. Or you could use a wooden tablet and cover it with clay or wax for writing on.

Most writers long, long ago wrote on pieces of broken clay pots. You would use a brush and ink to write on these pot pieces. Or you might write on papyrus, made from the stalk of a river reed. The stalks were mashed flat and smooth. They could be stuck together to make long rolls called scrolls. We get our word "paper" from papyrus. Or you might write on goat skin, sheep skin, or calf skin, which could be rolled into a scroll.

In this song, David says God wrote about him. He says he was in God's book even before he was born.

Psalm 139, by David

God, you know me.
You know when I sit down and when I get up.
You know what I'm thinking.
You know when I go out and when I lie down.
You know all my ways.
Even before I say a word, you know it all, God.

You go behind me and in front of me.
You put your hand on me.
It's wonderful.
But it's too much for me to understand.
Where can I go to get away from your Spirit?
Where can I run to get away from you?
I could go up into space, but you are there.
I could make a bed in the deep places below.
But you are there.
I could fly on the morning's wings.
I could land far beyond the sea.
But even there, your hand will lead me.
You right hand will hold on to me.
I might say, "I know the darkness will hide me."
But darkness is not dark to you.
Darkness is like light to you.
You made every part of me.
You put me together inside my mother.
I praise you, because the way you made me is wonderful.
Everything you do is wonderful.
I know that for sure.
My body was not hidden from you.
It was not hidden when you made me in the secret place.
You saw my body before it had a shape.
You planned all my days.
You wrote them in your book,
    even before I had lived one of them.
What you think about is so important to me, God!
I can't count all the things you think.
If I could, they would be more than pieces of sand.
When I wake up, I am still with you.
Look into me, God.
Know what's in my heart.
Test me, and know what I think about.
See if there is anything bad in me.
Lead me in the way that lasts forever.

WEEK 14

 Monday

Praise

The Hebrew word for the book of psalms is "Praises." When we "praise" someone, it's like we cheer for them. We tell them how great they are. When we praise God, we cheer for Him. We say how great He is.

The Hebrew people had a saying that we use today: "Hallelujah" (hal-lel-loo-yah). It means "Praise the Lord." The Hebrews called some of their songs the "Hallel" psalms, which means the praise songs.

David knew of many ways to praise God. He could bow or kneel to God. He could be quiet and spend a long time thinking about God. Or he could pray. In fact, David did all those things. But what we think of most when we think of David is his songs. He used his music and songs to praise and thank God, like in this song:

Psalm 145, by David

I will bow before you, my God the King.
I will praise you every day.
I will worship your name forever.
No one can understand how great God is.
God is loving and kind.
He does not get angry quickly.
He is full of love.
God is good to everyone.
He is kind to everything he made.
God keeps all his promises.
He treats everything he made with love.
He holds up everyone who falls.
God is right in everything he does.
He is loving.
He is near everyone who calls to him.
He gives good things to people who look up to him.
He hears their cry and saves them.
God watches over people who love him.
But he gets rid of sinful people.
My mouth will cheer for God.
Let everyone praise his name forever.

 Tuesday

Weather

Winter was wet and cold in the land of Canaan. The sea would get wild and windy and very cold. Sea travel was dangerous in winter. To the north on Mount Hermon, there was snow all winter. Sometimes snow and ice fell on Jerusalem. To the south, around the Salt Sea, the weather was not as cold. Kings built palaces there so they could move south in the winter.

Summer was hot and dry. In early morning, wind from the hot desert would begin to blow across the land. Rain usually did not fall in the summer. So plants and rivers dried up and the ground got dusty. In the south, the weather was very hot. So kings moved back to their palaces in the north.

In David's time, there was no radio or weather channel, no internet, no weather reporters to tell what the weather was going be like the next day. Instead, people watched the sky and the clouds and felt the direction of the wind. They learned that if the sky was a bit red in the morning, the day would probably be stormy. If the sky was a bit red at sunset, the next day would probably be nice. If there was a ring around the moon at night, they knew it might rain.

In this song, the writer tells everything to praise God, even the weather:

Psalm 148

Praise God from heaven high above.
Praise him, all you angels.
Praise him, armies of heaven.
Praise him, sun and moon.

Praise him, you stars that shine.
Praise him, you high heavens.
Let everything God made praise him.
He said the word, and they were made.
He set them in their places forever.
Praise God from the earth.
Praise him, you great sea life.
Praise him, you deep ocean.
Praise him, lightning and hail.
Praise him, snow and clouds and
 storm winds that do what he says.
Praise him, you mountains and hills.
Praise him, fruit trees and cedar trees.
Praise him, you wild animals and cows.
Praise him, small animals and birds that fly.
Praise him, kings and all nations,
 princes and all you rulers.
Praise him, young men and women,
 old men and children.
Let them all praise God.
His name should be most important.
He is greater than the earth and sky.
He gave his people a strong king.
He is the one they cheer for.
They are close to his heart.
Praise God.

 Wednesday

Dancing

The Hebrew people often danced. Men danced in one group, and women danced in another group. They skipped and whirled. Dancing was one way they worshiped God and celebrated His loving care for them. When their army won a great battle, they danced. When they had a holiday, they danced. When someone got married, they danced. Sometimes people would celebrate with a parade, and they would dance in the parade. That's what happened when God's ark box was brought back to Jerusalem. King David threw off his king's cloak and danced in the parade.

In this song, the writer tells people to dance as they praise God:

Psalm 150

Praise God in his mighty heavens.
Praise him for the powerful things he has done.
Praise him for how great he is.
Praise him with horns and harps.
Praise him with tambourines and dancing.
Praise him with flutes and with cymbals that crash.
Let everything that lives praise God!

 Thursday

Chariots

A chariot was a small cart with two wheels. It was pulled by horses and was only big enough for two or three people to stand in. The back of a chariot was usually open. Most chariots were made out of wood and leather. But some were made of metal.

Chariots were often used for hunting. Kings also rode around in chariots, especially in parades through their cities. But chariots were really made for fighting. A soldier could stand in a chariot, and while it was moving, he could shoot his arrow or throw his spear. If there were three soldiers in a chariot, one would hold a shield to protect the others. Sometimes chariots drove as fast as they could toward the enemy to scatter the enemy fighters.

In this song David says he does not trust in chariots, but in God. He also prays that his people will wave their flags in God's name. Flags were sometimes called banners. When an army or a large group of travelers was getting together, a banner was held high to show them where to meet. A banner was also held up when a battle was about to start.

Psalm 20, by David

I pray that God will answer you when you are sad.
I pray that God will guard you and send you help.
I pray that he will remember the worship gifts
   you gave him.
I pray that God will give you what you wish for.
I pray that he will make your plans work out.
I pray that we'll shout and be glad when you win.
I pray that we'll wave our flags in God's name.
I pray that God will give you what you ask for.
God answers his people from heaven.
He saves them with his great power.
Some people trust in horses.
Some people trust in chariots.
They will fall.
But we trust in God.
We will stand strong.

 Friday

Coming Back Home

Long ago, if an enemy fought your army and won, they might take you and your family and neighbors back to their land. Then they would send some of their people into your land. Your people and their people traded places. That way, the enemy could stay in control over you and your land. That's what happened to the Hebrews. After the time of David, many kings ruled over God's people. Then an enemy army came to fight the Hebrews. The enemy army won and took the Hebrews away from Canaan.

The Hebrews stayed in the enemy land for many, many years. At last, the king of that land let the Hebrews move back home. Some of the songs in the book of psalms were written then. The people were so glad to be going home that they sang about it. This is one of their songs:

Psalm 126

Enemies had taken us away.
   But God brought us back to Jerusalem.
   It was like a dream.
We were full of laughing and joy.
God has done great things for us.
   We are full of joy.
Give us what belongs to us, God.
   Let it be like rivers in the desert.
People may go out crying, holding seeds to plant.
   But they will come back with happy songs.
   They will bring the crops they have gathered.

WEEK 15

 Monday

Horses and Mules

Horses were fast. So horse riders were often used to carry messages. Horses could also pull wagons. In battles, they pulled chariots, or soldiers rode them. But Hebrews did not use horses much until the time of King David. Even then, only rich people owned horses. Horses were a sign of power. David's son King Solomon had as many as twelve thousand horses. He built special stables for them. He was the first Hebrew king to have a group of chariots pulled by horses for fighting.

A mule has a horse as its mother and a donkey as its father. The Hebrews used mules to carry packs, because they were better than horses at walking over rough mountain country. Mules were good for riding, too. In David's time, kings often rode mules. Sometimes soldiers rode mules in battles.

In this song, David says God told him not to be like a horse or mule that has to have a bit (a metal bar that goes in horse's mouth) and reins that the rider holds. The bit and reins help the rider control the horse.

Psalm 32, by David

People are happy when their sins are forgiven.
Their sins are erased.
People are happy when God throws away the list of their sins.
When I kept quiet about my sins, I felt terrible.
I cried all day.
Day and night, God, you tried to get me to listen.
My strength melted away
   like it does on a hot summer day.
Then I told you about my sins.
I didn't hide them.
I said, "I will tell God about my sins."
Then you forgave me.
So everyone who loves you should pray to you.
You are like a place for me to hide.
You keep me from trouble.
You give me songs about how you save me.
God says, "I will teach you how you should live.
I will watch over you.
Do not be like the horse or mule.
It doesn't understand at all.
It has to be led by a bit in its mouth.
It won't move without a harness and long reins."
People who do bad things have many troubles.
But the people who trust God
   will have God's love around them forever.
Everyone who obeys God should be glad.
Show your joy in God.
Sing if your heart is sinless.

 Tuesday

Carrying Water

In David's time, there were no plastic water bottles. There were no glass bottles. Instead, you would carry water, milk, or wine in a clay jar or in a pouch made of animal skin, also called leather. Your leather pouch might be made of sheep skin or goat skin, oxen or donkey skin. It would have a spout for pouring, and the opening would be tied closed or plugged with a clay stopper.

Clay jars came in different sizes. You might have a large jar for holding water at home and a small jar for carrying water on your shoulder from the well. An even smaller jar might be used to dip water from the large jar and pour it into your stew pot or over hands for washing. Some jars had more than one spout.

If you traveled, you might carry a traveler's jar, a clay bottle with flat sides and two handles around its neck. It looked a bit like what we would call a canteen.

In this song, Korah's family talks about being thirsty for God like a deer is thirsty for water:

Psalm 42, by Korah's Family

My soul is like a deer that is thirsty for water.
My soul is thirsty for the living God.
When can I meet with God?
My tears are all that I have for food day and night.
Why are you sad, my soul?
Why am I troubled inside?
I will trust in God.
I will praise him, because he saves me.
Deep water calls when the waterfall roars.
I feel like waves have splashed over me.
God sends his love every day.
At night he sends his song.
It's a prayer to God.
I say to God, "Why did you forget me?
Why must I go around crying, held back by my enemies?"
My body hurts as my enemies tease me.
They say, "Where is your God?"
Why are you sad, my soul?
Why am I troubled inside?
I will trust in God.
I will praise him, because he
   saves me.

 Wednesday

Neighbors

From the beginning, God told the Hebrews to respect their neighbors. Many of the laws God gave them were about how to treat neighbors. At first, the Hebrews lived in tents. Their neighbors lived in tents not too far from them. But there was space between the tents. When they began living in towns, neighbors were closer. Often the walls of one house joined the walls of the next house, like apartments and condos do now. Streets were not like ours. They were just very narrow alleys between some of the houses. There were no garbage collectors to come and take trash away. But they also did not have as much garbage as we have now. That's a good thing, because trash often piled up in the street.

With people living so close together, it was easy for your neighbor to bother you. It was also easy for you to bother your neighbor. So it was important to remember one of God's most important rules: love your neighbor. (Leviticus 19:18)

In this song, David says he will not let people tell lies about their neighbors:

Psalm 101, by David

I will sing about your love, God.
I will sing about how fair you are.
I will be careful to live a life without sin.
I will walk in my house with a sinless heart.
I won't let my eyes see anything bad.
I hate what people do when they don't love you.
I won't let them near me.
I will stay away from people who sin in their hearts.
Some people might tell lies about their neighbors.
But I will tell those people to be quiet.
I will not stay around anyone
    who has a proud look and a proud heart.
I will look for people I can trust.
I'll let them live with me.
No one who lies will live in my house.
Every morning I will find all the sinful people.
I will not let them live in God's city.

 Thursday

Eating

The Hebrews had two main meals every day. The first was breakfast. Soon after you got up in the morning, you would get yourself a piece of flat bread and cheese. You might also get some dried fruit or olives. Sometimes you wrapped your bread around the cheese and fruit or olives to eat it. That worked best for the men and boys, who would often leave for their work, eating their breakfast as they went. During the day, they might stop for a drink or a piece of fruit, but they did not eat lunch like we do.

Mothers and girls spent a big part of their day making the food for that night's supper. If the family did not grow what they needed, they would buy their fruits and vegetables at the market. The market place might be near the town gate. The sellers often sat on the ground with their fruits and vegetables next to them. Some women bought bread from bakers, but others made their own bread.

Most people did not eat much meat. Their dinner was usually a pot of vegetable stew. At supper time, they put the pot on a rug on the floor, and everyone sat around the pot. They scooped up the stew with a piece of bread. After that, they would eat fruit and drink wine. The wine was often mixed with water.

This song says God gives food to people who trust Him. The Hebrews believed that, and they always said thanks before eating.

Psalm 111

I will thank God with all my heart.
I will praise him with people who do what is right.
What God does is great and powerful.
He is good and kind.
He is fair and right.
He gives food to people who trust him.
He remembers his promises forever.
You can trust his way.
God's name is special. It's the best!
Treat God as the most important one.
That's how to begin to be wise.
Everyone who obeys God understands.
Praise God forever.

 Friday

Guards in the Night

In David's time, while you were asleep, a guard stayed awake and watched to make sure everyone was safe. Sometimes the guard was a soldier. If you lived in the city, the guard would stand on top of the city wall and watch. If you were out in the country, the guard might be a soldier or just a man from your group. But these guards did not stay up all night. They took turns watching. Night time was made of three "watches" in David's time. If you were a guard, you might take the beginning of the watches, right after the sun went down. Or you might have the middle watch, in the middle of the night. Or you might have the morning watch, which started sometime after midnight and ended when the sun came up.

The guard's job was to wake everyone up if he saw danger. In the country, danger might be robbers or wild animals. Inside the city, danger might be an enemy army coming or a fire starting in the city. But most of the time, there was no danger. Everything was quiet. A guard could get bored. He would look forward to going home, where he could sleep. If he was a guard on the morning watch, he might want the sun to hurry and come up.

In this song, the writer says he waits for God more than guards wait for the morning:

Psalm 130

I cry to you, God. Hear my voice.
Be kind to me.
If you kept track of our sins,
 no one could be good enough for you.
But you forgive. So we look up to you.
I wait for God more than guards wait for the morning.
Hope in God, because God's love never ends.
He can save his people from their sin.

WEEK 16

 Monday

Babies

When a baby was born in David's time, it was washed and then rubbed with salt. People thought the salt would make the baby's skin firm. Then the mother would put the baby on a square of cloth, fold the corners around the baby and wrap strips of cloth around it. Sometimes these strips were colorful or they had designs on them. This was called swaddling the baby. It kept the baby's arms straight by its side. People thought that helped the baby's arms grow straight and strong. Many times during the day, the mother would unwrap the cloth around the baby and rub olive oil on its skin. Then she would dust the baby with myrtle leaves that had been ground into a powder.

With the baby wrapped this way, the mother could easily carry it on her back in a cloth sling. Some mothers folded their cloak to make a sling to carry the baby. At night, the mother could hang the sling from a roof beam like a hammock. She could swing it to rock the baby. Or she could set two strong sticks into the ground and hang the sling from these. This made a cradle for the baby.

In this song, David talks about how God's care makes him feel as good as a well-fed baby whose mother is taking good care of him:

Psalm 131, by David

My heart is not proud, God.
I don't worry about things
    that are too big for me to understand.
I don't worry about things
    that are too wonderful for me.
My soul is still and quiet
    like a well-fed baby with its mama.
Put your hope in God now and forever.

 Tuesday

Blind and Needy

Long ago, it was common for people to lose their sight and become blind. Some were born blind. But most blind people lost their sight because they got an eye sickness. They did not know about germs. God had told the Hebrews they were supposed stay clean and wash their hands before eating. But much of their work was with their hands, outdoors, in the dust and dirt, or with animals. If they rubbed their eyes, they might get germs in their eyes. The sun was also very strong and they had no sunglasses to protect their eyes. If they lost their sight, someone had to lead them around. They could not work, so they had to beg people for money or food.

Widows and orphans might also have to beg. If the father of a family died, the family did not have a way to get their food or have a home. The mother was called a widow. The children were called fatherless or orphans.

God told the Hebrews to take care of blind people and widows and orphans. God is sometimes called the Father of the fatherless. In this song, the writer says God takes care of people who can't see and children who have no fathers:

Psalm 146

My soul, praise God.
I will cheer for him all my life.
I will sing praise to him as long as I live.
Don't trust the leaders of the land to save you.
They are only people.
When they die, their plans become nothing.
But good things come to people who let God
   be their helper.
Their hope is in God.
He is the one who made heaven and earth and sea.
He is the Lord.
He always keeps his promises.
He takes care of people who are not treated right.
He gives food to people who are hungry.
He helps people who can't see
   so they're able to see again.
He lifts up people who feel pushed down by trouble.
He loves everyone who does what's right.
God watches over strangers.
He cares for children who have no fathers.
He takes care of women who have no husbands.
But he gives sinful people trouble.
God is King forever.
Cheer for God!

 Wednesday

Perfume

People had no deodorant in David's time, so they often used perfume. Here are some of the perfumes they used:

Aloe came from a tree. Sometimes kings used it to make their clothes smell good.

Balsam probably came from the mastic tree. When a branch of this tree was cut, a yellow, good-smelling sap came out.

Cinnamon came from the bark of a big tree. Cinnamon oil was put on one of the Hebrews' worship tents to make it smell good.

Gum was a yellow or yellow-brown sap that came from some plants. One of the darker gums came from rock roses. It smelled so sweet it was used for perfume.

Myrrh came from sap too. It was put on clothes to cover odors.

Nard cost a lot of money. It came from the roots of a special plant and smelled very good.

People who made perfume were called perfumers. Sometimes they made perfume by squeezing oil out of the plant. Other times they dropped flower seeds and petals into hot oil so the oil would soak up the sweet smell. Sometimes they spread fresh flower petals on a layer of animal fat. The fat would soak up the smell.

In this song, Korah's family says the king's robes smell good with perfume:

Psalm 45, A Love Song by Korah's Family

My heart is happy about telling my poems to the king.
My voice is like a pen that belongs to a good writer.
King, you are the best of all men.
God will bring good to you forever.
Hang your sword by your side.
Ride out for truth and for what is right.
Ride out and win.
Do wonderful things.
Let your sharp arrows shoot your enemies.
Let the nations fall before you.
You will be king forever.
You will be fair when you rule your kingdom.
You love what's right and hate what's wrong.
So God has made you great.
He has let joy flow over you.
Your robes smell sweet with perfume.
Music from beautiful palaces makes you happy.
Many princesses are with you.
The queen is at your right hand.
She is dressed in gold.
Listen and think about it, princess.
Forget about your home far away.
The king is so happy with your beauty.
Look up to him.
People will bring you gifts.
Rich people will want to meet you.
The princess is bright and beautiful in her room.
Her gown is made of gold.
She is led to the king in her beautiful gown.
Her friends follow her with joy.
They are glad to go to the king's palace.
Your sons will grow up to rule many lands.
People will remember you.
All nations will praise you forever.

 Thursday

Joy Songs

The Hebrew people had lots of holidays, which means "holy days." Like we do at our holidays, people of David's time ate special foods and spent time with family and friends. Every month, at the time of the new moon, they celebrated and blew their trumpets and brought special gifts to the worship house for God. At the Holiday of Tents, each family made huts of twigs and branches to help them remember how God kept them safe on their travels. The Holiday of Harvest was a happy time, full of giving thanks to God for sending rain and good crops.

There were many other holidays. Most of them were like parties. Often there was music and dancing, clapping and shouting. Many of the psalms were written to be songs of joy. In this song, Korah's family tells people to clap and shout for joy:

Psalm 47, by Korah's Family

Clap your hands, all you people.
Shout to God with joy.
God, the Lord Most High, is wonderful.
He is the great King of all the earth!
He puts other nations under us.
He chose to give us a good land to live in.
We are his people, and he loves us.
Sing praises to God.
Sing praises to our King, sing praises!
God is the King of all the earth.
Sing a song of praise to him.

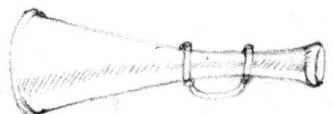

 Friday

Sharing Stories

Long ago in David's time, there were no televisions, no internet, no radios. There were not many books. But there were stories. Grandfathers and grandmothers would tell stories. Fathers and mothers would tell stories. Aunts and uncles would tell stories. They would tell stories while they were working together. They would tell stories while they traveled. They would tell stories at dinner time and at night after supper. Many of the stories the Hebrew people told were true stories about God and how He had helped them. The children would listen to those stories over and over again. And when they grew up, they would tell the same stories to their own children. That's the way stories were remembered. Some of these stories were written down, and we can read them in the Bible even today.

The worship day and holidays were special times to tell stories of how God helped His people. Sometimes the Hebrews set up landmarks to remind them of their stories. These were places they marked to show where God had done something special. The landmark could be one tall stone or a pile of stones. Children would see the stones and ask what they were and why the stones were there. Then the older people would tell the story of how God helped the Hebrew people there.

Some of the psalms tell these stories. Songs made it easier to remember what God did for them. This song talks about how fathers from long ago told about God. Then it says we will tell God's story too.

Psalm 44:1-8

Our fathers from long ago told us what you did.
You planted your people in their land.
    You made your people grow strong.
They didn't win the land by swords.
    They didn't win by their strong arms.
The power of your right hand won for them.
    The light of your face was on them, and they won.
    It's all because you loved your people.
You are my King and my God.
    It's by your name that we win.
I don't trust in my bow and arrow.
    My sword does not make me win.
You make us win over our enemies.
We talk about how great God is all day long.
    We will praise your name forever.

Sources

<u>Bible Encyclopedia: A First Reference Book</u>. Etta Wilson and Sally Lloyd Jones. Joshua Morris, 1995.

<u>Eerdmans' Family Encyclopedia of the Bible</u>, Pat Alexander, ed. Grand Rapids: Eerdmans, 1978.

<u>Everyday Life in Bible Times</u>. Margaret Embry. Nashville: Thomas Nelson, 1994.

<u>Growing Up in Bible Times</u>, Margaret Embry. Nashville: Thomas Nelson, 1995.

<u>Holman Bible Dictionary</u>, Trent C. Butler, ed. Nashville: Holman, 1991.

<u>How They Lived in Bible Times</u>, Graham Jones and Richard Deverell. Ventura, CA: Gospel Light, 1992.

<u>Lands of the Bible</u>, Nigel Hepper. Nashville: Thomas Nelson, 1995.

<u>The Life and Times of Jesus the Messiah</u>: New Updated Edition, Alfred Edersheim. np: Hendrickson, 1993.